CONTENTS 5B

UNIT 1

Do You Want to Feed the Rabbits?

Look. There are rabbits.

They're cute. They have long ears and short tails.

Do you want to feed the rabbits?

Yes, I do.

CHECK 04

1 What does the boy say about the rabbits? ⓐ ☐ ⓑ ☐

2 What does the girl want to do? ⓐ ☐ ⓑ ☐

Practice

Ⓐ Listen and write the letter. 05

Ⓑ Listen and repeat. 06

Do you want to ride a horse?	Yes, I do.	No, I don't.

Listen & Talk

A Listen, number, and circle. 07

YOUR TURN

B Check, write, and say.

- [ ] see koalas
- [ ] take a walk
- [ ] go to the beach
- [ ] feed the cows

Do you want to ____________?

Yes, I do. / No, I don't.

Write & Talk

Ⓐ Write, listen, and talk. 08

feed them	want	pandas
vacation	go on a trip	

Tim: What do you want to do this ____________?

Ann: I want to ______________.

I want to go to China.

Tim: What do you want to do there?

Ann: I want to see __________.

Tim: Do you __________ to ____________?

Ann: Sure, I do. It will be fun.

Ⓑ Listen and check. Then say. 09

1

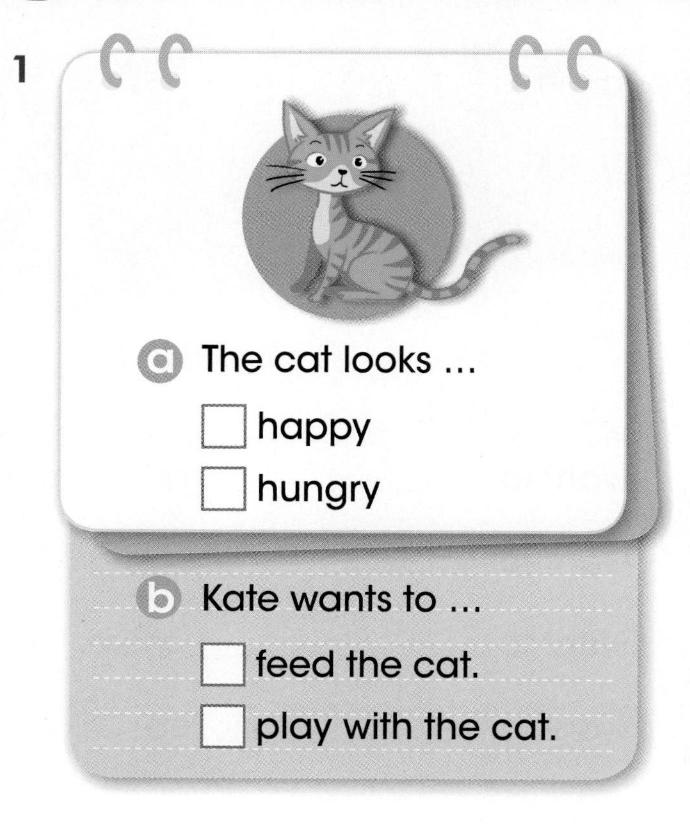

ⓐ The cat looks …

- ☐ happy
- ☐ hungry

ⓑ Kate wants to …

- ☐ feed the cat.
- ☐ play with the cat.

2

ⓐ Ron is …

- ☐ tired
- ☐ busy

ⓑ He wants to …

- ☐ sleep at home.
- ☐ take a walk.

Reading

Ⓐ Listen and read. 10

Tomorrow is Saturday.

What do you want to do tomorrow?

I want to go to the aquarium.

I want to see dolphins.

I don't want to stay home.

Do you want to see jellyfish, too?

Yes, I do. They're beautiful.

I want to take many pictures there.

Sounds fun. Have a good time.

Thank you.

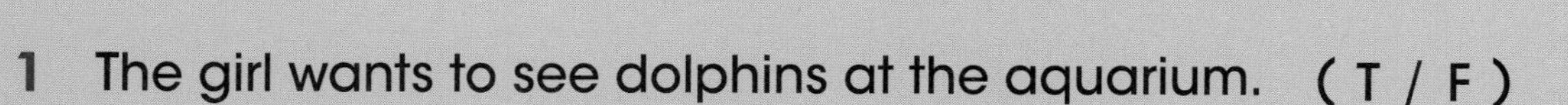

1 The girl wants to see dolphins at the aquarium. (T / F)

2 The girl doesn't want to see jellyfish. (T / F)

Ⓑ Look and write.

I want to ...

- go on a trip
  ⇣
- go to Australia
  ⇣
- see kangaroos
  eat steak

I want to ______________ this summer.

I want to ______________.

I want to ______________ there.

I want to ______________, too.

Build Up

Ⓐ Listen and repeat. 11

want(s) to ~

Do you want to take a walk?
I want to go to the beach.
I don't want to see pandas.

Does he want to ride a horse?
He wants to ride a bike.
He doesn't want to eat fish.

Ⓑ Complete the sentence.

ride a horse	feed the cows
stay home	jump rope
go to the aquarium	go on a trip

1

Do you want ____________________?

2

Does she want ____________________?

3

I don't want ____________________.

I want ____________________.

4

She ____________________.

5

He doesn't ____________________.

Check-Up

A Listen and match. 12

3

4

B Listen and choose. 13

1

O

a b

2

3

4

C Listen and circle. 14

1 David wants to take a walk / see kangaroos in Australia.

2 Nora wants to go to the beach / swim at the beach .

D Look and write.

1

A: __________ you want __________ see __________?

B: Yes, I do.

2

A: __________ she want to ______________?

B: No, she doesn't.

3

A: __________ do you __________ to do this weekend?

B: I want to ______________.

E Write and say.

1

A: ________________________________

B: No, I don't.

2

A: ________________________________

B: Yes, I do.

UNIT 2
It Has a Pink Heart
Mini Talk Look and listen. 17
Excuse me.
I lost my umbrella.
What does it look like?
It has a pink heart.
Is this yours?
No, my umbrella
is green.
Oh, that's mine!
Lost & Found
CHECK 18
1 What does the boy's umbrella look like? a b
2 Is the boy's umbrella green? a b

Practice

A Listen and write the letter.  **B** Listen and repeat. 

A: I can't find my bag.
B: What does it look like?
A: It has a big pocket.

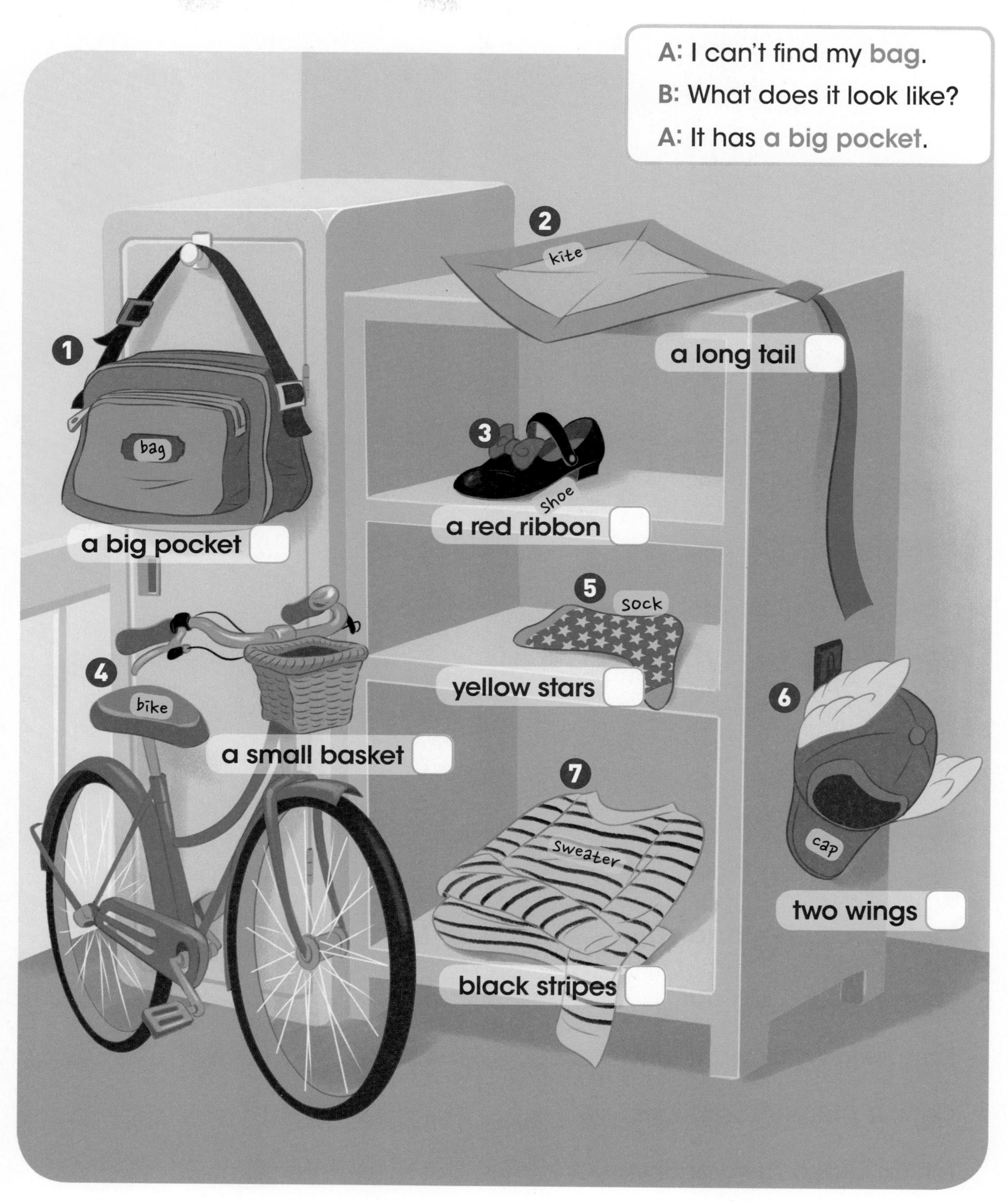

Listen & Talk

A Listen and choose. 21

1

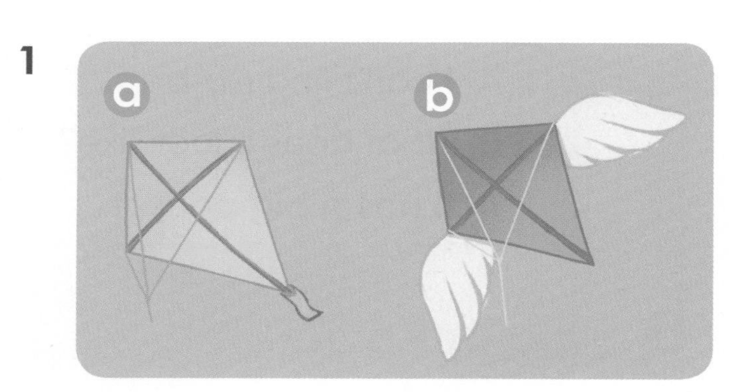

2

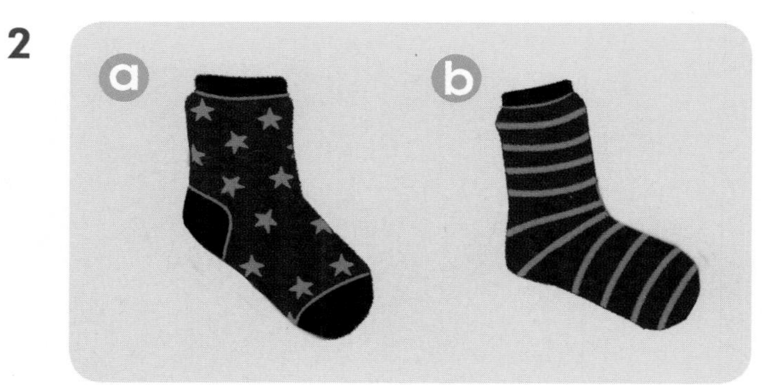

3

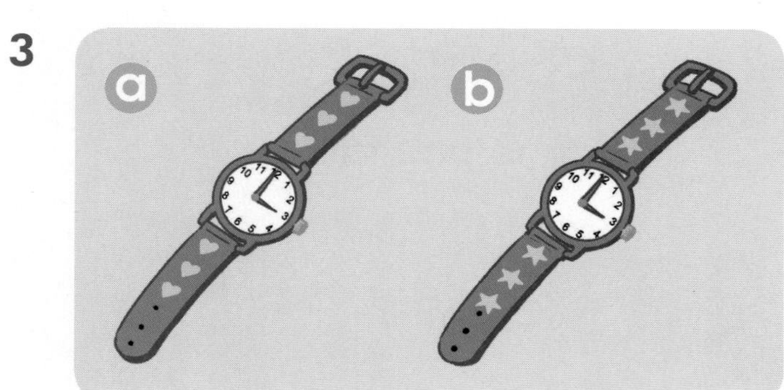

4

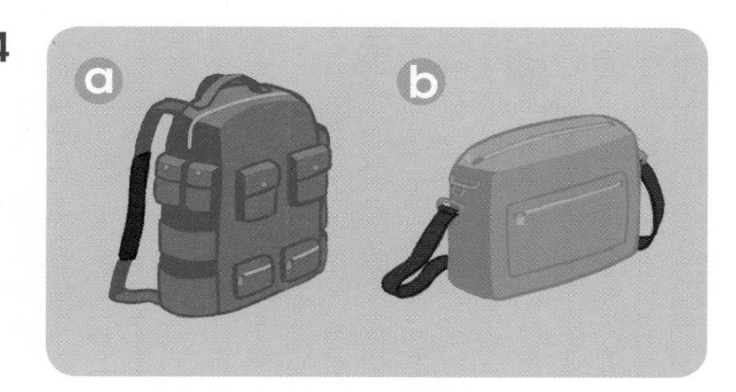

5

6

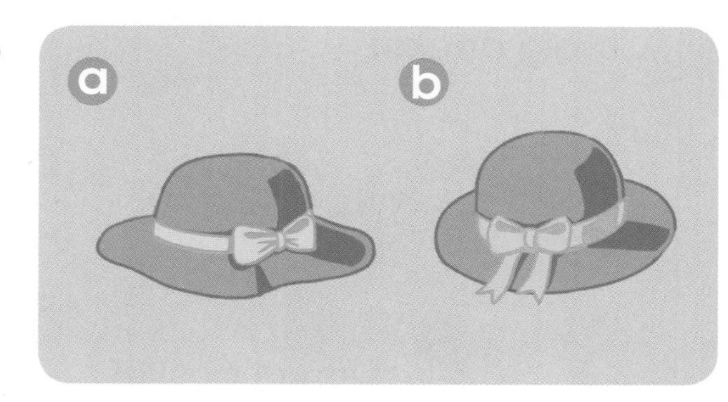

B Check, write, and say.

- [ ] bag / red / a big star
- [ ] umbrella / yellow / a pink heart
- [ ] jacket / blue / red stripes
- [ ] shirt / green / two pockets

Write & Talk

Ⓐ Write, listen, and talk. 22

big what has
mine like

Sue: I bought a new backpack.

Tony: __________ does it look like?

Sue: It's pink. It has a __________ star.

Tony: Oh, my backpack __________ stars, too. I __________ stars.

Sue: Is this your backpack?

Tony: Yes, it's __________.

Ⓑ Listen, check, and draw. Then say. 23

ⓐ
- The cup is ☐ blue. ☐ green.
- It has ☐ small hearts. ☐ white stars.

ⓑ

ⓐ
- Kevin's shoes are ☐ green. ☐ brown.
- They have ☐ two yellow stripes. ☐ three yellow stars.

ⓑ

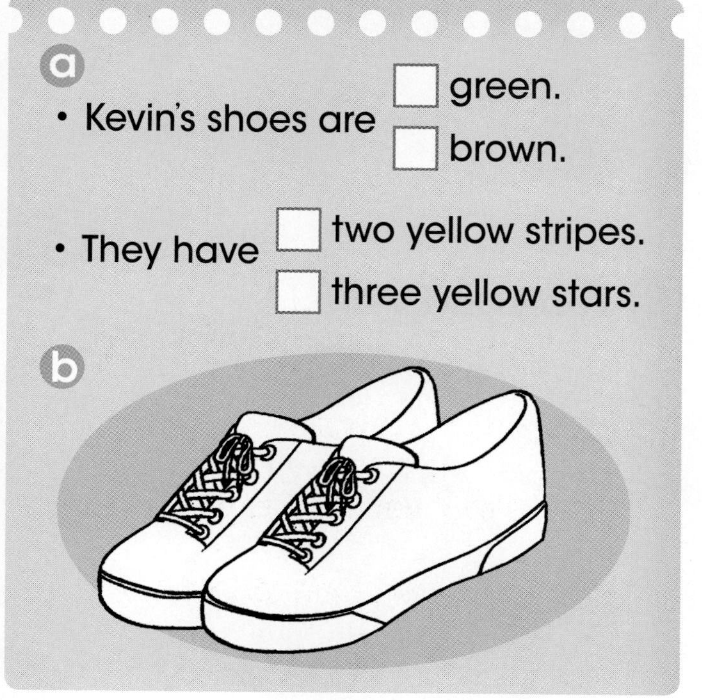

Reading

A Listen and read. 

Do you like dinosaurs?

They lived on earth long ago.

Look at this picture.

Can you find a T. rex?

It has a long tail and short arms.

It has sharp teeth, too.

It is a fast and strong dinosaur.

The T. rex is my favorite dinosaur.

1 A T. rex has two wings. (T / F)

2 A T. rex is a strong dinosaur. (T / F)

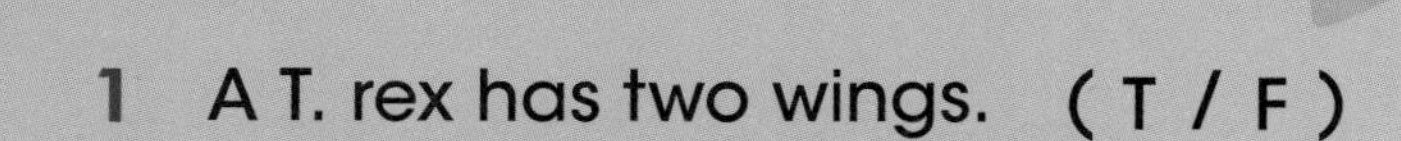

B Look and write.

Look at my cat, Mimi.

She is ____________.

She has ________________.

She has ________________.

She is a lovely cat.

Ⓐ Listen and repeat. 25

two small pockets

two	small	pockets
many	black	stripes
big	blue	ribbon

- The bag has two small pockets.
- My shirt has many black stripes.
- Her hat has a big blue ribbon.

Ⓑ Complete the sentence.

1 

My sweater has a ____________________.
(heart / big / green)

2 

The jacket has ____________________.
(pockets / big / two)

3 

Lisa's cap has ____________________.
(two / wings / white)

4 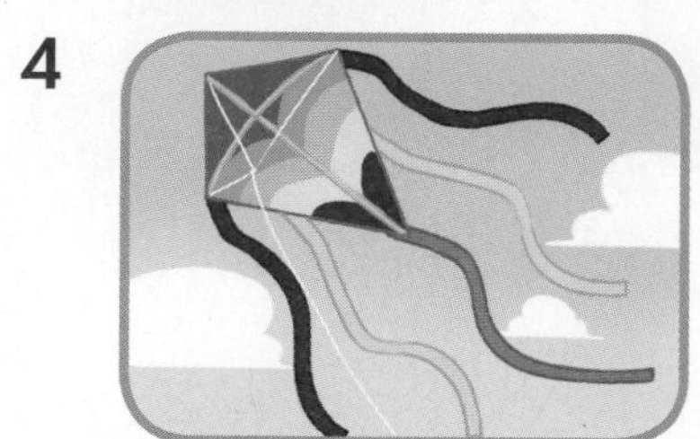

The kite has ____________________.
(tails / many / long)

5 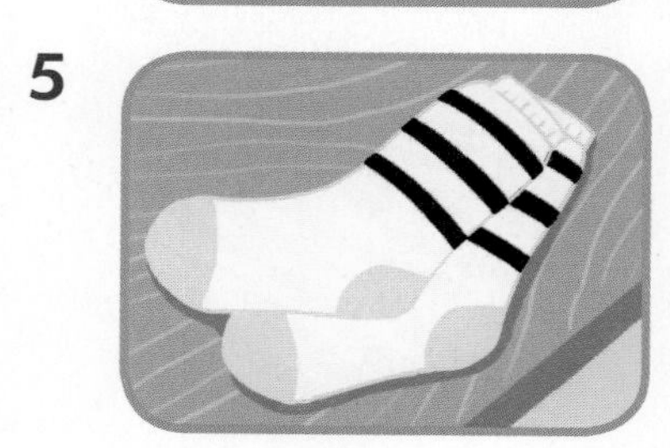

These socks have ____________________.
(stripes / black / three)

Check-Up

Ⓐ Listen and number. 26

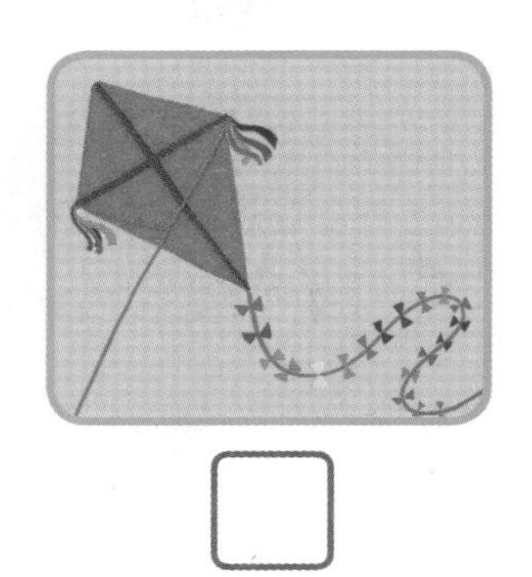

Ⓑ Listen and match. 27

1 
2 
3 
4 

Ⓒ Listen and circle. 28

1 The girl's bag has a yellow ribbon / green ribbon .

2 The boy's cap has white stripes / black stripes .

D Look and write.

a yellow heart	blue	two pockets
small basket	red	look like

1

A: I can't find my sock.

B: What does it look like?

A: It's ___________. It has ____________________.

2

My bag is pink.

It has ____________________.

3

A: I bought a new bike.

B: What does it _____________?

A: It's ___________. It has a _______________.

E Write and say.

1

My umbrella is green.

It has ________________________.

2

My kite is ___________.

It ______________________________.

Review 1

A Read and write.

Do you want to feed the cat? Yes, I do. It has a long tail.

1

2

B Read and write the letter.

1 A: Do you want to ride a horse? B: Yes, I do. ☐

2 A: Do you want to see pandas? B: Yes, I do. ☐

3 A: Do you want to go to the aquarium? B: No, I don't. ☐

4 A: Do you want to jump rope? B: No, I don't. ☐

C Look, write, and circle.

1 

A: What ________ it look like?

B: It's yellow. It has (black stripes / black stars).

2 

A: What does it ________ like?

B: It has (a long tail / a big pocket).

3 

A: What does it ________?

B: It's red. It has (a big heart / a small basket).

UNIT 3 I Had a Pajama Party

Mini Talk Look and listen. 31

CHECK 32

1 What did Kate do last weekend? ⓐ ☐ ⓑ ☐

2 How was the party? ⓐ ☐ ⓑ ☐

Practice

A Listen and write the letter. 33

B Listen and repeat. 34

A: I joined a ski camp.
B: How was it?
A: It was fun.

Listen & Talk

Ⓐ Listen, match, and check. 35

1 

2 

3 

4 

5 

- ☐ great ☐ boring
- ☐ exciting ☐ great
- ☐ boring ☐ fun
- ☐ great ☐ boring
- ☐ fun ☐ exciting

YOUR TURN

Ⓑ Check, write, and say.

- ☐ the game / exciting
- ☐ the movie / boring
- ☐ the party / great
- ☐ the book / interesting

Write & Talk

Ⓐ Write, listen, and talk. 36

saw	went	what
how	exciting	

Bob: _________ did you do last weekend?

Tina: I _________ to the science museum.

Bob: What did you do there?

Tina: I _________ a 4D science movie.

Bob: _________ was the movie?

Tina: It was _________.

Ⓑ Listen, check, and circle. Then say. 37

Reading

Ⓐ Listen and read. (38)

Chris

I went camping with my family last weekend.

We swam at the lake together.

We made a campfire at night.

It was great.

Lisa

I watched a basketball game

with my friends.

The game was very exciting.

Our team won the game.

We ate some popcorn, too.

We had a fun time.

1 Chris swam at the beach last weekend. (T / F)

2 Lisa's team won the basketball game. (T / F)

Ⓑ Look and write.

fun

a barbecue party

great time

visited my friend

I ______________ last weekend.

We had ______________.

The party was very ______________.

I had a ______________.

Build Up

A Listen and repeat. 39

How was / were ~?

- A: How was the game?
  B: It was fun.
- A: How were the cookies?
  B: They were delicious.

B Complete the dialog.

1

A: How was the pajama party?

B: ________ ________ fun.

2

A: ________ ________ the trip?

B: It was great.

3

A: How ________ the museum?

B: ________ was boring.

4

A: ________ ________ the fries?

B: They were salty.

5

A: How were the comic books?

B: ________ ________ fun.

Check-Up

A Listen and number. 40

B Listen and mark O or X. 41

1

2

3

4

C Listen and choose. 42

1 Judy ____________ last weekend.

ⓐ went camping ⓑ had a party ⓒ watched a soccer game

2 How was the book?

ⓐ It was boring. ⓑ It was great. ⓒ It was fun.

D Look and write.

how boring how was great
went fishing had a barbecue party

1

A: We ______________________.

B: ________ was it?

A: It was fun.

2

A: I ____________ last weekend.

B: How was it?

A: It was ________.

3

A: I joined a ski camp.

B: ____________ the camp?

A: It was ________.

E Write and say.

1

A: I ______________________.

B: How was it?

A: ______________________

2

A: I ______________________.

B: ______________________

A: It was fun.

UNIT 4

I Have a Stomachache

Mini Talk Look and listen. 45

Dad, let's have some ice cream.

Don't eat too fast.

What's wrong?

I have a headache.

Toilet

I have a stomachache.

CHECK 46

1 What did they eat? ⓐ ☐ ⓑ ☐

2 Does the boy have a headache? ⓐ ☐ ⓑ ☐

Practice

Ⓐ Listen and write the letter. 

Ⓑ Listen and repeat. 

A: What's wrong?
B: I have a cold.
A: Drink some warm water.

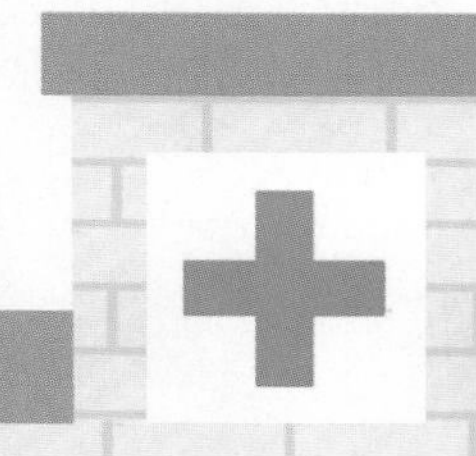

1 

cold / drink some warm water

2 

headache / get some rest

3 

fever / take some medicine

4 

runny nose / take some medicine

5 

stomachache / go and see a doctor

6 

toothache / go and see a dentist

Listen & Talk

Ⓐ Listen, number, and circle. 49

YOUR TURN Ⓑ Check, write, and say.

- ☐ cold / drink some warm water
- ☐ fever / take some medicine
- ☐ toothache / go and see a dentist
- ☐ headache / get some rest

Write & Talk

have	medicine	look
go to bed	headache	

Ⓐ Write, listen, and talk. 50

Mom: You __________ sick. What's wrong?

Alex: I have a __________.

I __________ a fever, too.

Mom: That's too bad. Take this __________

and __________ early.

Alex: Okay, Mom.

Ⓑ Listen, circle, and check. Then say. 51

1

2

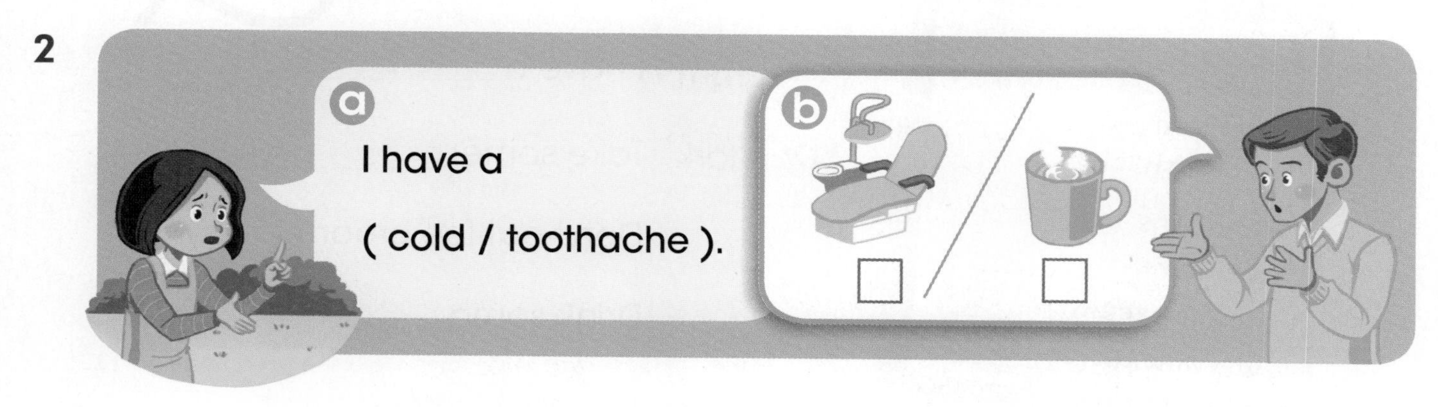

Reading

Ⓐ Listen and read. 52

Ask Dr. Clark

Dr_Clark.com

Elsa

Hello, I'm Elsa. I'm twelve years old.
I feel sick. I have a fever.
I have a runny nose, too.
Do I have a cold?

Dr. Clark

Yes, Elsa. You have a cold.
Take some medicine and get some rest.
Drink some warm water, too.
Don't go outside today.

Elsa

Okay, I will. Thank you.

1 Elsa has a stomachache. (T / F)

2 Elsa will take some medicine. (T / F)

Ⓑ Look and write.

Tom: I have a ______________.

Dr. Clark: Take some ______________.

Don't eat ice cream today.

Drink some ______________.

Build Up

Ⓐ Listen and repeat. 53

Ⓑ Look and complete.

look have looks has

1

He ________ tired.

He ________ a lot of homework.

2

I feel sick today.

I ________ a fever.

3

Cathy ________ a camera.

The camera ________ old.

4

A: You ________ sad. What's wrong?

B: My puppy ________ a stomachache.

5

A: He ________ sick. What's wrong?

B: He ________ a toothache.

Check-Up

Ⓐ Listen and choose. 54

1 

ⓐ ⓑ ⓒ

2 

ⓐ ⓑ ⓒ

3 

ⓐ ⓑ ⓒ

4 

ⓐ ⓑ ⓒ

Ⓑ Listen and match. 55

1 

2 

3 

4 

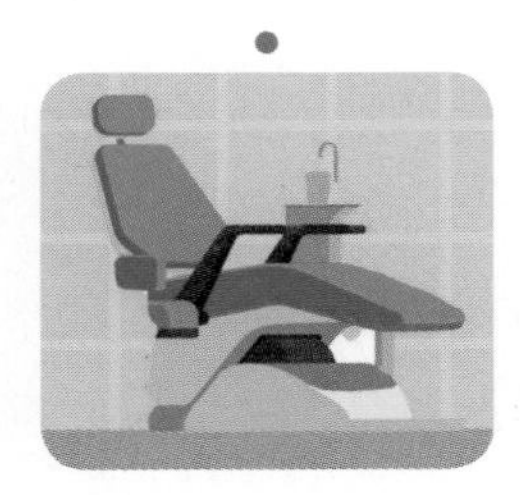

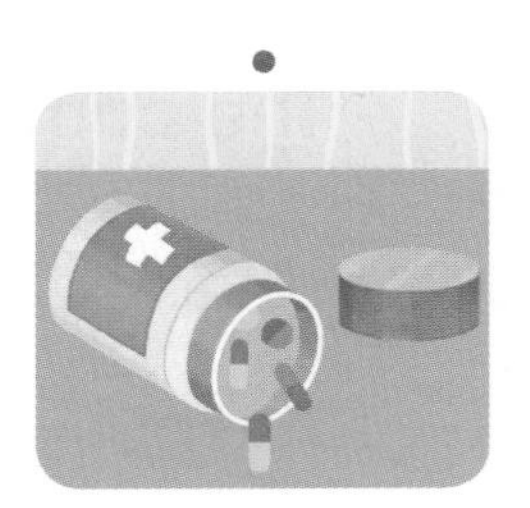

Ⓒ Listen and choose. 56

1 ⓐ Jane has a stomachache.

ⓑ Jane has a toothache.

2 ⓐ The boy will go and see a dentist.

ⓑ The boy will go and see a doctor.

D Look and write.

1

A: What's ____________, Amy?

B: I have a ____________.

A: Take some ____________.

2

A: You ____________ sick. What's wrong?

B: I have a ____________.

A: Go and see a ____________.

3

A: I ____________ a cold, Dad.

B: That's too bad. Drink some ____________ water and get some ____________.

E Write and say.

1

A: What's wrong?

B: ______________________________

2

A: I have a runny nose.

B: ______________________________

Review 2

Ⓐ Read and write.

It was great.	I have a cold.	I went fishing.

B Look, write, and circle.

read a comic book saw a movie
had a barbecue party

1

A: I ______________________.

B: How was it?

A: It was (fun / boring).

2

A: I ______________________.

B: How was it?

A: It was (fun / boring).

3

A: I ______________________.

B: How was it?

A: It was (exciting / boring).

C Look and write.

What's wrong?

1 I have a ______________.

2 I have a ______________.

3 I have a ______________.

4 I have a ______________.

UNIT 5

What Season Do You Like?

Mini Talk Look and listen. 59

It's very hot today.
I don't like summer.

What season do you like?

I like fall.
What about you?

I like summer because
my birthday is in summer.

1 Does the girl like summer? ⓐ ☐ ⓑ ☐

2 What season does the boy like? ⓐ ☐ ⓑ ☐

Practice

A Listen and write the letter. 

B Listen and repeat. 

What season do you like?

I like spring because I can see many flowers.

Listen & Talk

A Listen and match. (63)

1 

2 

3 

4 

YOUR TURN

B Check, write, and say.

- ☐ spring / see many flowers
- ☐ summer / eat watermelon
- ☐ fall / go camping
- ☐ winter / make a snowman

I like __________ because I can

____________________.

Write & Talk

season winter fall
winter sports favorite

A **Write, listen, and talk.** 64

Alex: What's your __________ season?

Kate: My favorite season is __________.

I like to go camping.

What __________ do you like?

Alex: I like __________ because I can

enjoy ______________.

I like to go skiing.

Kate: We have winter vacation, too.

B **Listen and check. Then say.** 65

1

a
Anna likes ...
☐ winter ☐ summer

b
☐ ☐

2

a
Jake likes ...
☐ spring ☐ fall

b
☐ ☐

Reading

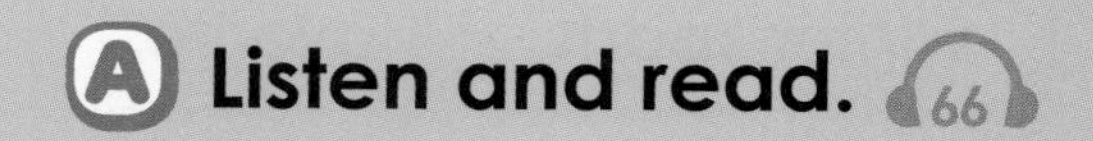

Ⓐ Listen and read. 66

This is Minho. He lives in Korea.

"It's August. It's summer now.

It's hot and sunny today.

I like summer because I can swim at the beach.

I like to go swimming."

This is Melisa. She lives in New Zealand.

"It's winter here. It's cold and snowy today.

I like winter because I can enjoy winter sports.

I like skiing and ice fishing.

Winter is my favorite season."

1 Minho likes to go swimming in summer. (T / F)

2 Melisa likes winter because it's snowy. (T / F)

Ⓑ Look and write.

Hi, I'm Paula. I live in __________.

It's spring now. It's __________________ today.

I like __________ because we ____________________.

A Listen and repeat. 67

because

I like summer **because** I can go swimming.

I don't like winter **because** the weather is cold.

B Read and match.

1

I like spring • • because it's too hot.

2

I don't like summer • • because it's boring.

3

We like Harry • • because I can have a picnic.

4

Bella likes basketball • • because she can jump high.

5

He doesn't like the book • • because he is funny.

Check-Up

Ⓐ Listen and match. 68

3

Ⓑ Listen and number. 69

Ⓒ Listen and choose. 70

1 Sam likes to ___________ in winter.

ⓐ go skiing ⓑ go skating ⓒ make a snowman

2 Bella's favorite season is ___________.

ⓐ spring ⓑ summer ⓒ fall

what season　have a picnic　season
see colorful leaves　see many flowers

D Look and write.

1

A: What season do you like?

B: I like fall because

I can ____________________.

2

A: What __________ do you like?

B: I like spring because

I can ____________________.

3

A: ______________ do you like?

B: I like spring because

I can ____________________.

E Write and say.

1

A: What season do you like?

B: __________________ because

______________ at the beach.

2

A: ____________________________

B: I like fall because I can go camping.

UNIT 6

Where Is the Bakery?

Mini Talk Look and listen. 73

CHECK 74

1 Where do they want to go? ⓐ ☐ ⓑ ☐

2 Did they buy some bread? ⓐ ☐ ⓑ ☐

Practice

Ⓐ Listen and write the letter. 75

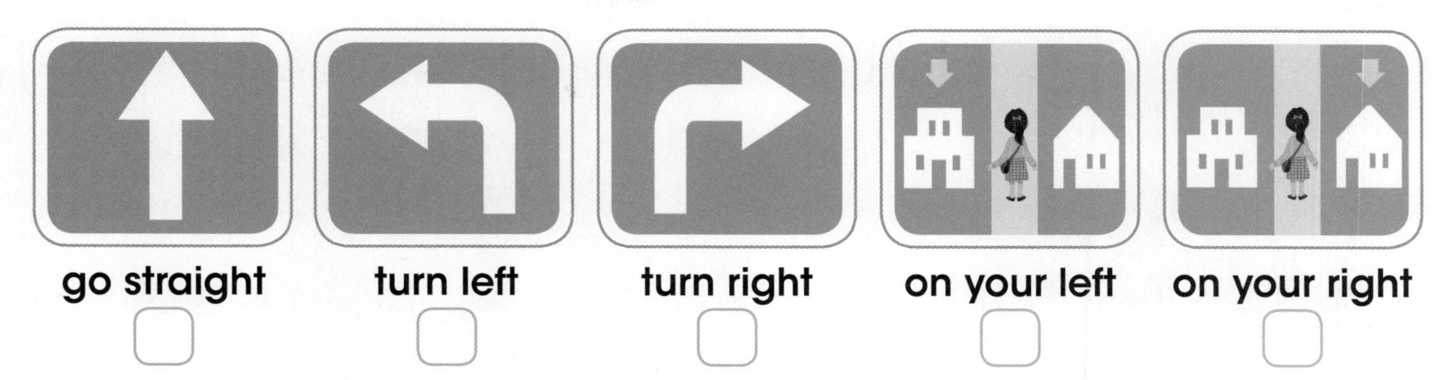

Ⓑ Listen and repeat. 76

Excuse me. Where is the library?

Go straight two blocks and turn left. It's on your left.

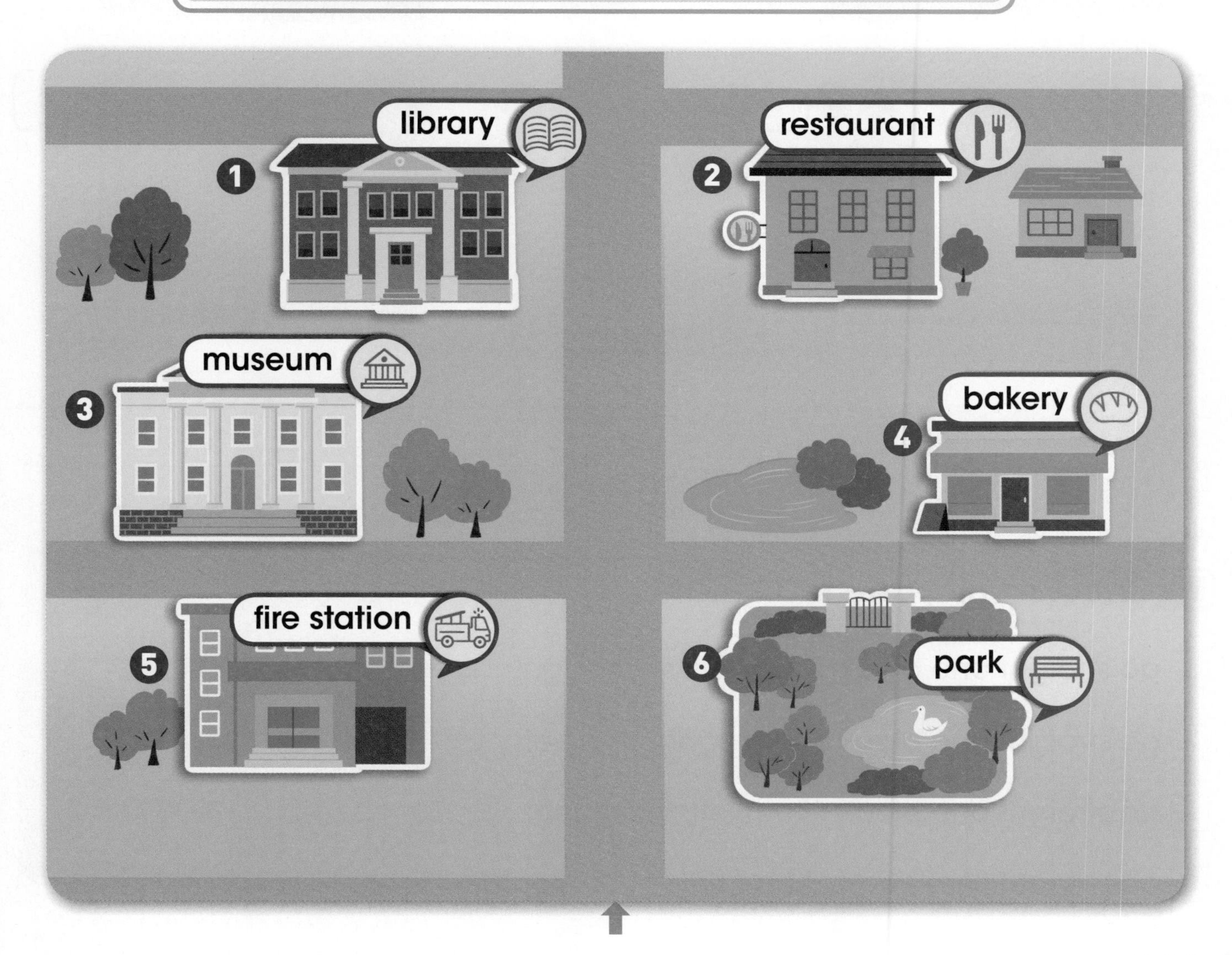

Listen & Talk

A **Listen and write the letter.** 77

1 a b ☐

2 a b ☐

3 a b ☐

4 a b ☐

5 a b ☐

6 a b ☐

_______________ and _______________.

It's on _______________.

YOUR TURN

B **Check, write, and mark. Then say.**

☐ go straight one block / turn left / your right

☐ go straight one block / turn right / your left

☐ go straight one block / turn left / your left

☐ go straight two blocks / turn right / your right

Write & Talk

A Write, listen, and talk. 78

how	turn	excuse
between	straight	

Ann: ________ me.

________ can I get to the post office?

Man: Go ________ and ________ right at the park. It's ________ the bank and the hospital.

Ann: Thank you.

Man: No problem.

B Listen and check. Then say. 79

Reading

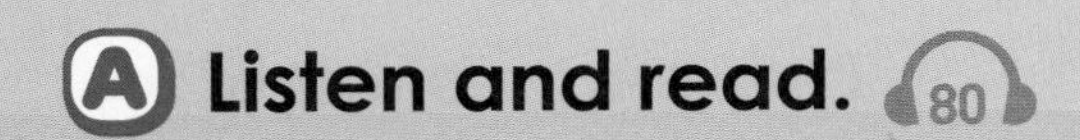

A new ice cream shop opens in town!

I want to go there tomorrow.

I love strawberry ice cream.

Where is the shop? Let's see.

Oh, it's here.

Go straight four blocks and turn right at the bank.

The ice cream shop is next to the supermarket.

I can walk there.

I'll go with my sister. She loves ice cream, too.

1 There is a new ice cream shop in town. (T / F)

2 The ice cream shop is next to the bank. (T / F)

Go __________ and turn __________ at the zoo.

It's on your __________.

It's __________ the flower shop.

A Listen and repeat. 81

next to / between / in front of / behind

B Complete the sentence.

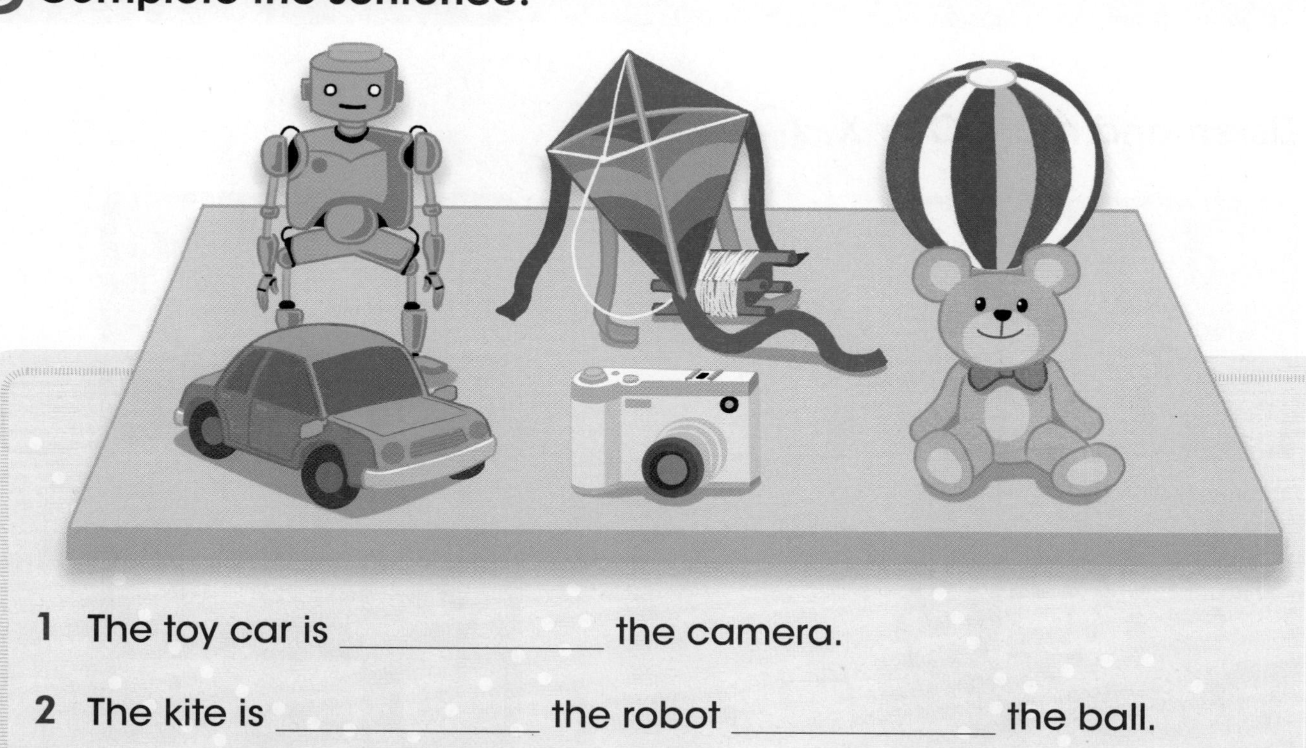

1 The toy car is ______________ the camera.

2 The kite is ______________ the robot ______________ the ball.

3 The teddy bear is ______________ the ball.

4 The robot is ______________ the toy car.

5 The kite is ______________ the ball.

6 The camera is ______________ the toy car ______________ the teddy bear.

Check-Up

Ⓐ Listen and number. 82

Ⓑ Listen and mark O or X. 83

1

2

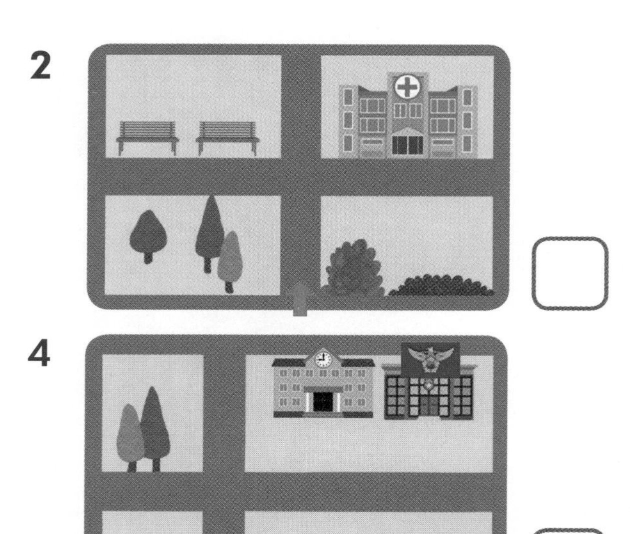

3

4

Ⓒ Listen and choose. 84

1 The park is __________ the shopping mall.

ⓐ next to ⓑ in front of ⓒ behind

2 The boy will go straight __________ and turn right.

ⓐ one block ⓑ two blocks ⓒ three blocks

D Look and write.

1

A: Where is the school?

B: Go straight ________ blocks and turn ________. It's on your ________.

2

A: Excuse me. Where is the post office?

B: Go straight ________ blocks and turn right. It's ________ your ________.

3

A: Where is the bakery?

B: Go straight one block and ________. It's ________ the restaurant.

E Write and say.

1

A: Excuse me. Where is the library?

B: ________________ and ________. It's on ________.

2

A: Where is the supermarket?

B: ________________ and ________. It's on ________.

Review 3

Ⓐ Read and write.

because I can swim at the beach　　What season do you like?
Go straight five blocks and turn left.

B Look and check.

1 I like winter
- ☐ because I can make a snowman.
- ☐ because I can enjoy winter sports.

2 I like spring
- ☐ because I can have a picnic.
- ☐ because I can see many flowers.

3 I like fall
- ☐ because I can eat watermelon.
- ☐ because I can go camping.

C Look and write.

1 A: Where is the flower shop?

B: Go straight ____________ and turn ________.

2 A: Where is the park?

B: Go straight ____________ and turn left.

3 A: Where is the restaurant?

B: Go straight ____________ and turn right. It's on your ________.

UNIT 7 Why Are You So Happy?

Mini Talk Look and listen. 87

CHECK 88

1 Is Mike happy? ⓐ ☐ ⓑ ☐

2 Why is Mike happy? ⓐ ☐ ⓑ ☐

Practice

(A) Listen and write the letter. 

(B) Listen and repeat. 

Why are you so happy?	I got a present.

1. happy / got a present ☐
2. sad / lost my cell phone ☐

3. excited / won the game ☐
4. upset / lost the game ☐

5. upset / broke my glasses ☐
6. worried / have a math test ☐

Listen & Talk

Ⓐ Listen and match. 91

1 • • excited •

2 • • worried •

3 • • upset •

4 • • happy •

5 • • sad •

YOUR TURN

Ⓑ Check, write, and say.

☐ excited / got a new bike

☐ sad / lost my watch

☐ worried / have an English test

☐ upset / broke my pencil case

Write & Talk

A Write, listen, and talk. 92

gray	lost	sad
find	look like	

Alex: What's wrong, Kate?

Why are you so __________?

Kate: I __________ my cat, Coco.

Alex: That's too bad.

What does she __________?

Kate: She's __________. She has green eyes.

Alex: Don't worry.

Let's __________ her together.

B Listen and check. Then say. 93

1 Jane is ...

ⓐ

☐ excited ☐ worried

ⓑ Why?

☐ She got a new bike.

☐ She has a test.

2 Tom is ...

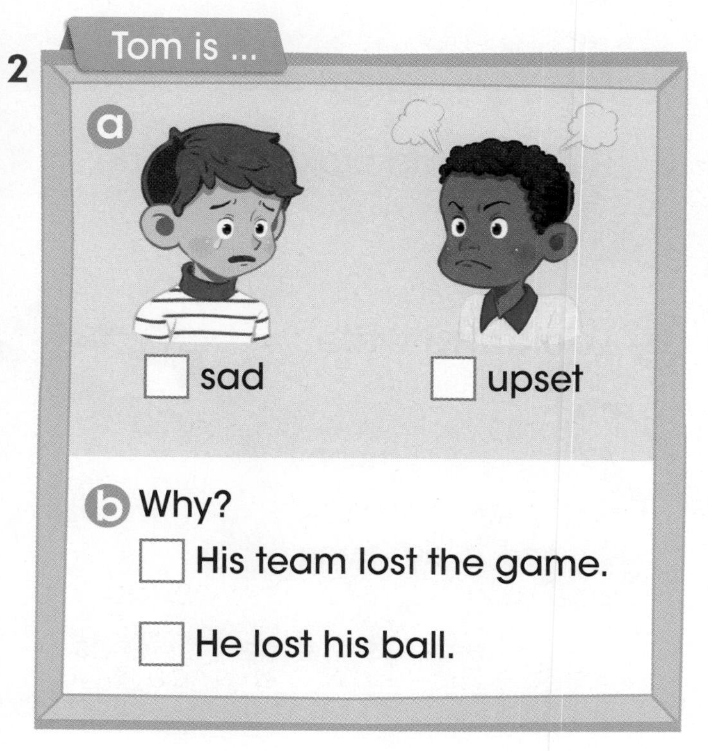

ⓐ

☐ sad ☐ upset

ⓑ Why?

☐ His team lost the game.

☐ He lost his ball.

Reading

Ⓐ Listen and read. (94)

Friday, September 4th

I'm so excited today.

Why am I so excited?

I got a new drone. It's red and black.

I want to fly it. I can't wait.

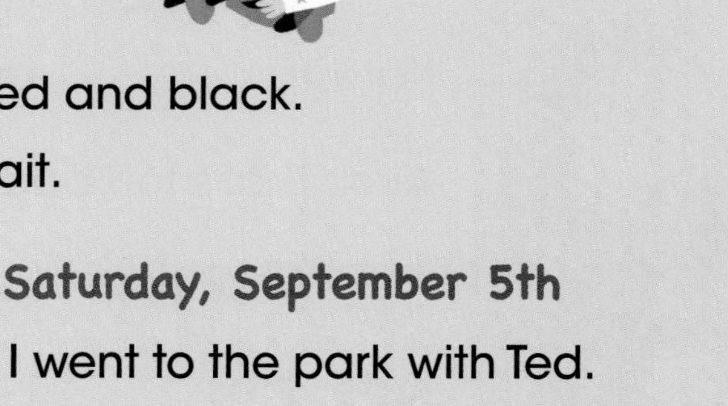

Saturday, September 5th

I went to the park with Ted.

He flew my drone and broke it.

I was upset.

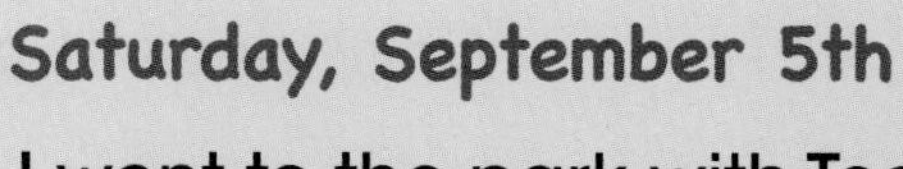

Sunday, September 6th

My drone is okay.

Dad fixed it. I'm happy now.

Thank you, Dad!

1 The girl is excited because she got a new drone. (T / F)

2 The girl's dad broke the drone. (T / F)

Ⓑ Look and write.

happy

joined a ski camp

made some new friends

I'm so ________ today.

I ________________.

I can ski now.

I ____________________, too.

Build Up

A Listen and repeat. 95

because I got a present

I'm happy because I got a present.

B Complete the sentence.

1

I'm happy because

I ______________________.

2

I'm sad because

I ______________________.

3

She's upset because

she ______________________.

4

He's excited because

he ______________________.

5

We're worried because

we ______________________.

6

I'm happy because

I ______________________.

made a new friend	have a math test	broke her glasses
won the game	got a new bike	lost my dog

Check-Up

A Listen and number. 96

B Listen, circle, and match. 97

1 upset / worried

2 sad / excited

3 happy / sad

4 excited / upset

C Listen and choose. 98

1 The girl is happy because she ________________.

ⓐ got a drone ⓑ got a present ⓒ got a new bike

2 Molly is upset because her brother ________________.

ⓐ broke her robot ⓑ lost her robot ⓒ helped her

D Look and write.

1

A: ________ are you so excited?

B: I ________ a new __________.

A: It's nice.

2

A: ________ are you so ________?

B: I have a __________ tomorrow.

A: Don't worry. I can help you.

3

A: What's wrong?

B: I'm sad ________ my team ________ the game.

E Write and say.

1

A: Why are you so excited?

B: ______________________________

2

A: ______________________________

B: My cat broke my cup.

UNIT 8 I'm Going to Go Shopping

Mini Talk Look and listen. 101

CHECK 102

1 What is the girl going to do? ⓐ ☐ ⓑ ☐

2 What is the boy going to do? ⓐ ☐ ⓑ ☐

Practice

A Listen and write the letter. 

B Listen and repeat. 

What are you going to do this afternoon?

I'm going to see a musical.

see a musical ☐

get a haircut ☐

visit the museum ☐

practice the piano ☐

finish my art project ☐

plant trees ☐

go to the bookstore ☐

go sledding ☐

Listen & Talk

A Listen and mark O or X. 105

1

2

3

4

5

6

YOUR TURN

B Check, write, and say.

☐ go camping	☐ this afternoon
☐ meet my friend	☐ this evening
☐ watch a tennis game	☐ tomorrow
☐ practice the violin	☐ this weekend

I'm going to ______________

______________.

Write & Talk

nice	going	what
go camping		join

A Write, listen, and talk. 106

Tim: ________ are you going to do tomorrow?

Sue: I'm __________ to ______________ with my friends.

Tim: That's a __________ plan.

Sue: We're going to ride a boat and make a campfire.

Do you want to __________ us?

Tim: Of course.

B Listen and check. Then say. 107

1

a

☐ tomorrow

☐ after school

b

☐ ☐ ☐

2

a

☐ this afternoon

☐ on Sunday

b

☐ ☐ ☐

Reading

A Listen and read. 108

What is Victor going to do this weekend?

He's going to finish his science project.

He has a good idea.

"I'm going to make a star map.

I'm going to watch the stars at night."

It's Saturday night.

There are many stars in the sky.

He watches the stars and draws the map.

The map looks wonderful.

1 Victor is going to finish his art project. (T / F)

2 Victor is going to make a star map. (T / F)

B Look and write.

Amy has a nice plan.

She is going to __________ tomorrow afternoon.

She is going to __________ with him.

They are going to __________ after the musical.

Ⓐ Listen and repeat. 109

be going to

We are going to make cookies this afternoon.

I am going to meet my friends tomorrow.

He is going to go camping this weekend.

Ⓑ Complete the sentence.

1

I / visit the museum

→ I am going to ______________________ tomorrow.

2

she / get a haircut

→ ______________________ this afternoon.

3

he / fly his drone

→ ______________________ this afternoon.

4

we / go to the airport

→ ______________________ today.

5

I / have a party

→ ______________________ next weekend.

Check-Up

Ⓐ Listen and choose. 110

1 

2 

3 

4 

Ⓑ Listen and choose. 111

1 

2 

3 

4 

Ⓒ Listen and circle. 112

1 Tina is going to have a party / go shopping tomorrow.

2 Max is going to get a haircut / go sledding this weekend.

D Look and write.

1

A: What are you ____________ this weekend?

B: I'm going to ________________.

A: That's a nice plan.

2

A: What are you ___________ do tomorrow?

B: I'm going to ______________ with Tom.

A: Have a good time.

3

A: ________ is she going to do this afternoon?

B: __________________ to the bookstore.

E Write and say.

1

A: What are you going to do tomorrow?

B: ______________________________

2

A: ______________________________ this weekend?

B: I'm going to plant trees.

Ⓐ Read and write.

I'm going to watch a baseball game.

That's a nice plan.

Why are you so happy?

B Circle and match.

1 

2 

3 

1 Why are you so (sad / happy)? •

2 Why are you so (excited / worried)? •

3 Why are you so (sad / excited)? •

• I got a present.

• I lost my cell phone.

• I won the game.

C Look and write.

visit the museum get a haircut
practice the piano

1 

A: What are you going to do tomorrow?

B: I'm going to ________________.

2 

A: What is he going to do on Sunday?

B: He's ________________________.

3 

A: What is she going to do after school?

B: She's ________________________.

Reading Plus

A Baseball Day 113

Tim, Jade, and I went to the ball park on Saturday.

We watched a baseball game together.

The game was so boring.

But the chicken and hotdogs were delicious.

We went to the Park Store.

It's in the ball park.

Tim bought a new cap. It has a big star.

Jade bought a T-shirt.

It's white and has blue stripes.

I bought a brown baseball glove. I like it.

We had a fun time.

Main Idea

1 This story is about ______________.

ⓐ delicious food

ⓑ a day at the ball park

ⓒ going to the market

ⓓ Jade's new T-shirt

Comprehension

2 How was the game?

ⓐ It was fun.
ⓑ It was exciting.
ⓒ It was boring.

3 What did Tim buy?

ⓐ a cap
ⓑ a ball
ⓒ a glove

4 What does Jade's new T-shirt look like?

ⓐ It has a star.
ⓑ It has stripes.
ⓒ It's brown.

Writing Practice

How was the chicken? ···› It was delicious.

1 How was the trip?

···› It ______________________________. (great)

2 How were the comic books?

···› ______________________________ (fun)

Fun Plans 114

It's Saturday morning.

I'm happy because it's sunny.

My family is going to go to the Animal Park today.

I want to see elephants and giraffes.

I want to feed them, too.

I'm going to visit my uncle this weekend.

He lives in Santorini.

I like Santorini because I can see pretty houses.

There is a beach next to my uncle's house.

I'm going to swim and dive there.

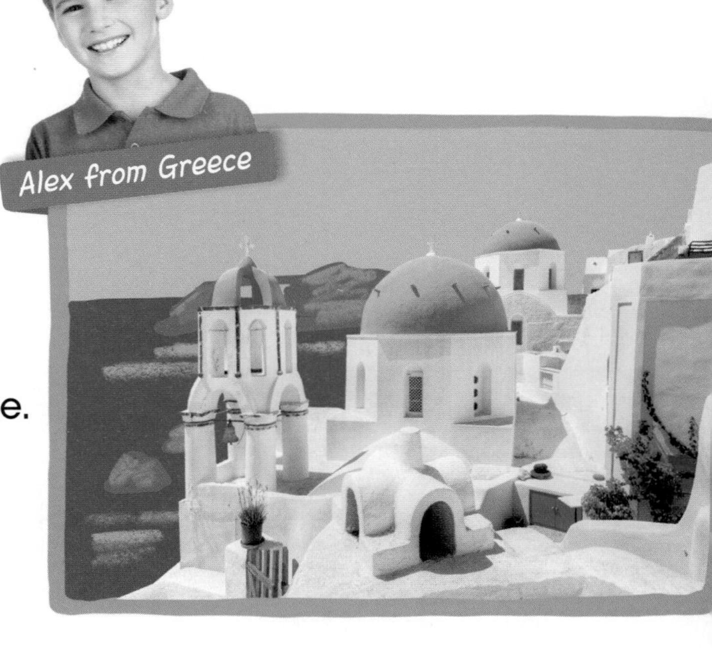

Main Idea

1 This story is about ________________.

ⓐ the weather

ⓑ zoo animals

ⓒ weekend plans

ⓓ summer vacation

Comprehension

2 Cora is going to go to ________________.

ⓐ the beach ⓑ her uncle's house ⓒ the Animal Park

3 Cora wants to ________________.

ⓐ go to the beach ⓑ feed the animals ⓒ swim and dive

4 Alex likes Santorini because he can ________________.

ⓐ feed the animals ⓑ see pretty houses ⓒ see giraffes

Writing Practice

I'm happy. / It's sunny. ···› I'm happy because it's sunny.

1 I like cats. / They are cute.

···› I like ____.

2 She is worried. / Her brother is sick.

···› ____

Regular Verbs

Base Form	Simple Past	Base Form	Simple Past
bake	baked	listen	listened
borrow	borrowed	open	opened
brush	brushed	pick	picked
clean	cleaned	plant	planted
climb	climbed	play	played
close	closed	push	pushed
cook	cooked	stay	stayed
cry	cried	study	studied
dance	danced	talk	talked
enter	entered	travel	traveled
exercise	exercised	use	used
help	helped	visit	visited
invent	invented	walk	walked
join	joined	wash	washed
jump	jumped	watch	watched

Irregular Verbs

Base Form	Simple Past		Base Form	Simple Past	
be (am/is/are)	was/were		make	made	
break	broke		meet	met	
bring	brought		put	put	
build	built		read	read	
buy	bought		ride	rode	
catch	caught		run	ran	
come	came		see	saw	
do	did		sing	sang	
draw	drew		sit	sit	
drink	drank		sleep	slept	
eat	ate		stand	stood	
fly	flew		swim	swam	
get	got		take	took	
go	went		win	won	
have	had		write	wrote	

Word List 5B

Unit 1 Do You Want to Feed the Rabbits?

dolphin ________
feed the cows ________
feed the sheep ________
go on a trip ________
go to the aquarium ________
jellyfish ________
jump rope ________
ride a horse ________
scared ________
see koalas ________
see pandas ________
stay home ________
take a walk ________

Unit 2 It Has a Pink Heart

backpack ________
black stripes ________
dinosaur ________
on earth ________
a long tail ________
a pink heart ________
a red ribbon ________
sharp ________
a small basket ________
strong ________
two wings ________
umbrella ________
yellow stars ________

Unit 3 I Had a Pajama Party

boring ________
exciting ________
fun ________
great ________
had a barbecue party ________
had a pajama party ________
joined a ski camp ________
made a campfire ________
read a comic book ________
swam at the lake ________
watched a baseball game ________
went fishing ________
went to a concert ________

Unit 4 I Have a Stomachache

cold ________
drink some warm water ________
fever ________
get some rest ________
go and see a dentist ________
go and see a doctor ________
headache ________
runny nose ________
sick ________
stomachache ________
take some medicine ________
toothache ________
wrong ________

Unit 5 What Season Do You Like?

eat watermelon ____________
enjoy winter sports ____________
fall ____________
go camping ____________
have a picnic ____________
make a snowman ____________
season ____________
see colorful leaves ____________
see many flowers ____________
spring ____________
summer ____________
swim at the beach ____________
winter ____________

Unit 6 Where Is the Bakery?

behind ____________
between ____________
go straight ____________
in front of ____________
next to ____________
one block ____________
turn left ____________
turn right ____________
two blocks ____________
your left ____________
your right ____________

Unit 7 Why Are You So Happy?

broke my glasses ____________
excited ____________
fixed ____________
got a present ____________
happy ____________
have a math test ____________
lost my cell phone ____________
lost the game ____________
made a new friend ____________
sad ____________
upset ____________
won the game ____________
worried ____________

Unit 8 I'm Going to Go Shopping

after school ____________
finish my art project ____________
get a haircut ____________
go sledding ____________
go to the bookstore ____________
map ____________
plant trees ____________
practice the piano ____________
see a musical ____________
this afternoon ____________
this weekend ____________
visit the museum ____________
wonderful ____________

Syllabus 5B

Unit 1 Do You Want to Feed the Rabbits?

Structures	Vocabulary		Grammar
• Do you want to ride a horse?	feed the rabbits	go on a trip	want(s) to ~
Yes, I do. / No, I don't.	ride a horse	take a walk	
• What do you want to do this vacation?	stay home	go to the aquarium	
I want to go to China.	feed the sheep	jump rope	
• It will be fun.	see pandas		**Reading**

Unit 2 It Has a Pink Heart

Structures	Vocabulary		Grammar
• I can't find my bag.	a pink heart	a small basket	two small pockets
What does it look like?	a big pocket	yellow stars	
It has a big pocket.	a long tail	two wings	
• I lost my umbrella.	a red ribbon	black stripes	
• Is this yours? - Yes, it's mine.			**Reading**
Review 1			

Unit 3 I Had a Pajama Party

Structures	Vocabulary		Grammar
• I joined a ski camp.	had a pajama party	watched a baseball game	How was ~? /
How was it?	joined a ski camp	fun	How were ~?
It was fun.	went fishing	exciting	
• What did you do last weekend?	read a comic book	boring	
• Did you join the ski camp?	had a barbecue party	great	
	went to a concert		**Reading**

Unit 4 I Have a Stomachache

Structures	Vocabulary		Grammar
• What's wrong?	cold	drink some warm water	look / have
I have a cold.	headache	get some rest	
Drink some warm water.	fever	take some medicine	
• You look sick.	runny nose	go and see a doctor	
• That's too bad.	stomachache	go and see a dentist	
• Don't go outside today.	toothache		**Reading**
Review 2			

Unit 5 What Season Do You Like?

Structures	Vocabulary		Grammar
• What season do you like? I like spring because I can see many flowers. • My favorite season is fall. • I like to go camping. • It's warm and nice.	see many flowers have a picnic eat watermelon swim at the beach	go camping see colorful leaves enjoy winter sports make a snowman	because **Reading**

Unit 6 Where Is the Bakery?

Structures	Vocabulary		Grammar
• Excuse me. Where is the library? Go straight two blocks and turn left. It's on your left. • It's next to the flower shop. • No problem.	go straight turn left turn right your left your right	one block two blocks next to between	next to / between / in front of / behind **Reading**
Review 3			

Unit 7 Why Are You So Happy?

Structures	Vocabulary		Grammar
• Why are you so happy? I got a present. • That's great. • That's too bad. • Don't worry. I can help you. • You look upset.	happy sad excited upset worried	got a present lost my cell phone won the game lost the game broke my glasses have a math test	because I got a present **Reading**

Unit 8 I'm Going to Go Shopping

Structures	Vocabulary		Grammar
• What are you going to do this afternoon? I'm going to see a musical. • Do you want to join us? • Have a good time. • That's a nice plan.	go shopping meet my friend see a musical get a haircut visit the museum	practice the piano finish my art project plant trees go to the bookstore go sledding	be going to **Reading**
Review 4			

5B

[11-12] Look and choose.

11

ⓐ It has a small basket.
ⓑ It has yellow stars.
ⓒ It has a big star.
ⓓ It has two wings.

12

ⓐ I want to stay home.
ⓑ I want to jump rope.
ⓒ I want to see pandas.
ⓓ I want to go to the aquarium.

[13-14] Look and mark O or X.

13 She has a runny nose. ☐

14 They had a barbecue party. ☐

[15-16] Read and choose.

15

A: ______________________
B: No, I don't.

ⓐ Do you want to go on a trip?
ⓑ What's wrong?
ⓒ How was it?
ⓓ What does it look like?

16

A: What's wrong?
B: I have a headache.
A: ______________________

ⓐ I want to take a walk.
ⓑ It has a big pocket.
ⓒ It was boring.
ⓓ Take some medicine.

[17-18] Look and write.

17

A: I ________ ________ last weekend.
B: How was it?
A: It ________ boring.

18

A: Do you want ________ ________ the sheep?
B: No, I ________.

[19-20] Unscramble the sentence.

19

A: What does your shirt look like?
B: ______________________________
(black / it / has / stripes / two / .)

20

A: I have a stomachache.
B: ______________________________
(see / go / and / a doctor / .)

115

Midterm TEST 5B

Institute ______
Name ______
Score /100

[1-2] Listen and choose.

1 ⓐ  ⓑ 

ⓒ  ⓓ 

2 ⓐ  ⓑ 

ⓒ  ⓓ 

3 Listen and choose.

ⓐ ⓑ ⓒ ⓓ

[4-6] Listen and choose.

4
A: ______
B: It's red. It has a big pocket.

ⓐ ⓑ ⓒ ⓓ

5
A: How was the game?
B: ______

ⓐ ⓑ ⓒ ⓓ

6
A: What's wrong?
B: ______

ⓐ ⓑ ⓒ ⓓ

[7-9] Listen and write the letter.

7 ☐ 8 ☐ 9 ☐

10 Listen and choose.

ⓐ  ⓑ 

ⓒ  ⓓ 

[13-14] Look and choose.

13

A: Why are you so happy?
B: ______________________

ⓐ I lost my cell phone.
ⓑ I got a present.
ⓒ My team won the game.
ⓓ My sister broke my robot.

14

A: Where is the flower shop?
B: ______________________

ⓐ It's behind the park.
ⓑ It's between the post office and the park.
ⓒ Go straight and turn right.
ⓓ It's in front of the post office.

[15-16] Read and choose.

15

I like fall __________ I can go camping.

ⓐ but ⓑ because
ⓒ at ⓓ to

16

A: __________ are you so sad?
B: I lost my bag.

ⓐ How ⓑ When
ⓒ Why ⓓ What

[17-18] Look and write.

17

A: Where is the bakery?
B: Go straight one block and turn __________.
It's __________ the restaurant.

18

A: Where is the hospital?
B: Go straight __________ blocks and turn left.
It's __________ your __________.

[19-20] Unscramble the sentence.

19

______________________ tomorrow?
(going to / what / you / are / do)

20

I like spring ______________________
______________________.
(many flowers / I / can / because / see)

Final TEST 5B

116

Institute

Name

Score /100

[1-2] Listen and mark O or X.

1

2

3 Listen and choose.

ⓐ 

ⓑ 

ⓒ 

ⓓ 

[4-5] Listen and choose.

4

ⓐ ⓑ ⓒ ⓓ

5

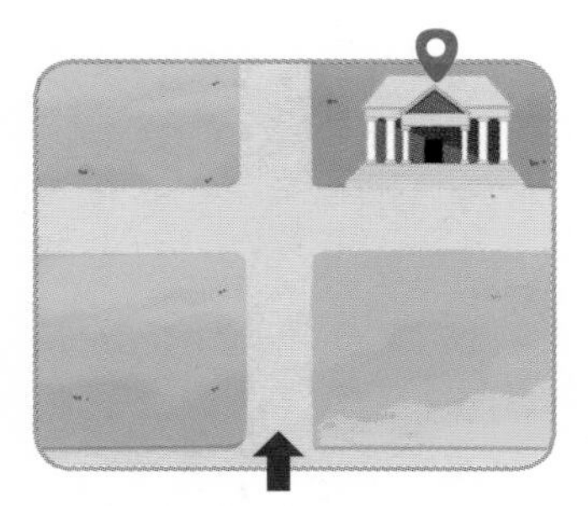

ⓐ ⓑ ⓒ ⓓ

[6-7] Listen and choose.

6 ⓐ ⓑ ⓒ ⓓ

7 ⓐ ⓑ ⓒ ⓓ

[8-10] Listen and match.

8 • • ⓐ 

9 • • ⓑ 

10 • • ⓒ 

[11-12] Read and write letter.

ⓐ 

ⓑ 

ⓒ 

ⓓ 

11 I like fall because I can see colorful leaves. ☐

12 I'm going to practice the piano. ☐

2nd Edition
LET'S GO
to the English World
5B

Word Book & Workbook

CHUNJAE EDUCATION, INC.

5B

Word Book

Do You Want to Feed the Rabbits?

Ⓐ Listen and repeat.  

ride a horse 말을 타다	**I want to** ride a horse**.** 나는 말을 타고 싶어.
stay home 집에 머물다	**Jill wants to** stay home**.** 질은 집에 머물고 싶어 해.
feed the sheep 양들에게 먹이를 주다	**Mike wants to** feed the sheep**.** 마이크는 양들에게 먹이를 주고 싶어 해.
see pandas 판다들을 보다	**We want to** see pandas**.** 우리는 판다들을 보고 싶어.
go on a trip 여행을 가다	**Do you want to** go on a trip**?** 너는 여행을 가고 싶니?
take a walk 산책을 하다	**Does he want to** take a walk**?** 그는 산책을 하고 싶어 하니?
go to the aquarium 수족관에 가다	**He doesn't want to** go to the aquarium**.** 그는 수족관에 가고 싶어 하지 않아.
jump rope 줄넘기를 하다	**We don't want to** jump rope**.** 우리는 줄넘기를 하고 싶지 않아.

B Read, write, and say.

☐ Read ☐ Write ☐ Say

1 ride a horse
말을 타다

2 stay home
집에 머물다

3 feed the sheep
양들에게 먹이를 주다

4 see pandas
판다들을 보다

5 go on a trip
여행을 가다

6 take a walk
산책을 하다

7 go to the aquarium
수족관에 가다

8 jump rope
줄넘기를 하다

Learn More

scared
무서워하는, 겁먹은

My brother is scared.
내 남동생은 겁을 먹었어.

dolphin
돌고래

We want to see dolphins.
우리는 돌고래들을 보고 싶어.

jellyfish
해파리

Do you want to see jellyfish?
너는 해파리들을 보고 싶니?

UNIT 2

It Has a Pink Heart

A Listen and repeat. 15 16

a pink heart 분홍색 하트 모양	It has a pink heart. 그것은 분홍색 하트 모양이 있어.
a big pocket 큰 주머니	It has a big pocket. 그것은 큰 주머니가 있어.
a long tail 긴 꼬리	The kite has a long tail. 그 연은 긴 꼬리가 있어.
a red ribbon 빨간색 리본	Her dress has a red ribbon. 그녀의 드레스는 빨간색 리본이 있어.
a small basket 작은 바구니	His bike has a small basket. 그의 자전거는 작은 바구니가 있어.
yellow stars 노란색 별 모양들	Jane's umbrella has yellow stars. 제인의 우산은 노란색 별 모양들이 있어.
two wings 두 개의 날개	My cap has two wings. 내 모자는 두 개의 날개가 있어.
black stripes 검은색 줄무늬	This jacket has many black stripes. 이 재킷은 많은 검은색 줄무늬가 있어.

(B) Read, write, and say.

☐ Read ☐ Write ☐ Say

1 a pink heart
분홍색 하트 모양
__________ __________ __________

2 a big pocket
큰 주머니
__________ __________ __________

3 a long tail
긴 꼬리
__________ __________ __________

4 a red ribbon
빨간색 리본
__________ __________ __________

5 a small basket
작은 바구니
__________ __________ __________

6 yellow stars
노란색 별 모양들
__________ __________ __________

7 two wings
두 개의 날개
__________ __________ __________

8 black stripes
검은색 줄무늬
__________ __________ __________

Learn More

umbrella 우산	**bag** 가방	**kite** 연	**shoe** 신발	**sock** 양말 한 짝
cap (야구) 모자	**bike** 자전거	**sweater** 스웨터	**watch** 손목시계	**hat** (챙 있는) 모자
on earth 지구상에	**backpack** 배낭, 책가방	**dinosaur** 공룡	**sharp** 날카로운	**strong** 강한

UNIT 3

I Had a Pajama Party

Ⓐ Listen and repeat. 29 30

had a pajama party 파자마 파티를 했다	I had a pajama party with my friends. 나는 내 친구들과 파자마 파티를 했어.
joined a ski camp 스키 캠프에 참가했다	Harry joined a ski camp. 해리는 스키 캠프에 참가했어.
went fishing 낚시를 하러 갔다	I went fishing with my brother. 나는 내 남동생과 낚시를 하러 갔어.
read a comic book 만화책을 읽었다	I read a comic book last Friday. 나는 지난 주 금요일에 만화책을 읽었어.
had a barbecue party 바비큐 파티를 했다	We had a barbecue party yesterday. 우리는 어제 바비큐 파티를 했다.
went to a concert 콘서트에 갔다	I went to a concert with James. 나는 제임스와 콘서트에 갔어.
watched a baseball game 야구 경기를 보았다	She watched a baseball game on TV. 그녀는 TV로 야구 경기를 보았어.
fun 재미있는	It was fun. 그것은 재미있었어.
exciting 흥미진진한	The movie was exciting. 그 영화는 흥미진진했어.
boring 지루한	The book was boring. 그 책은 지루했어.

Ⓑ Read, write, and say.

☐ Read ☐ Write ☐ Say

1 had a pajama party
파자마 파티를 했다

2 joined a ski camp
스키 캠프에 참가했다

3 went fishing
낚시를 하러 갔다

4 read a comic book
만화책을 읽었다

5 had a barbecue party
바비큐 파티를 했다

6 went to a concert
콘서트에 갔다

7 watched a baseball game
야구 경기를 보았다

8 fun
재미있는

9 exciting
흥미진진한

10 boring
지루한

Learn More

great
아주 좋은, 훌륭한

I had a great time.
나는 아주 좋은 시간을 보냈어.

swam at the lake
호수에서 수영을 했다

We swam at the lake together.
우리는 함께 호수에서 수영을 했어.

made a campfire
캠프파이어를 했다

We made a campfire at night.
우리는 밤에 캠프파이어를 했어.

UNIT 4

I Have a Stomachache

Ⓐ Listen and repeat. 43 44

cold 감기	I have a cold. 나는 감기에 걸렸어.
headache 두통	He has a headache. 그는 머리가 아파.
fever 열	I have a fever, too. 나는 열도 있어.
runny nose 콧물	She has a runny nose. 그녀는 콧물이 나.
stomachache 복통	Jake has a stomachache. 제이크는 배가 아파.
toothache 치통	Amy and I have a toothache. 에이미와 나는 이가 아파.
drink some warm water 따뜻한 물을 마시다	Drink some warm water, please. 따뜻한 물을 마시세요.
get some rest 휴식을 취하다	Get some rest at home. 집에서 휴식을 취해라.
take some medicine 약을 먹다	Take some medicine. 약을 먹어라.
go and see a doctor 병원에 가다	Go and see a doctor. 병원에 가라.
go and see a dentist 치과에 가다	Go and see a dentist. 치과에 가라.

B Read, write, and say.

☐ Read ☐ Write ☐ Say

1 cold
감기

2 headache
두통

3 fever
열

4 runny nose
콧물

5 stomachache
복통

6 toothache
치통

7 drink some warm water
따뜻한 물을 마시다

8 get some rest
휴식을 취하다

9 take some medicine
약을 먹다

10 go and see a doctor
병원에 가다

11 go and see a dentist
치과에 가다

Learn More

wrong 잘못된	What's wrong? 무슨 일이니? / 뭐가 잘못됐니?
sick 아픈	She feels sick. 그녀는 아파.
go to bed 잠자리에 들다	Go to bed early today. 오늘은 일찍 잠자리에 들어라.

UNIT 5

What Season Do You Like?

Ⓐ Listen and repeat. 57 58

see many flowers 많은 꽃을 보다	We can see many flowers in spring. 우리는 봄에 많은 꽃을 볼 수 있어.
have a picnic 소풍을 가다	I can have a picnic in spring. 나는 봄에 소풍을 갈 수 있어.
eat watermelon 수박을 먹다	We can eat watermelon in summer. 우리는 여름에 수박을 먹을 수 있어.
swim at the beach 해변에서 수영을 하다	I can swim at the beach in summer. 나는 여름에 해변에서 수영을 할 수 있어.
go camping 캠핑을 가다	We can go camping in fall. 우리는 가을에 캠핑을 갈 수 있어.
see colorful leaves 알록달록한 잎들을 보다	I can see colorful leaves in fall. 나는 가을에 알록달록한 잎들을 볼 수 있어.
enjoy winter sports 겨울 스포츠를 즐기다	We can enjoy winter sports in winter. 우리는 겨울에 겨울 스포츠를 즐길 수 있어.
make a snowman 눈사람을 만들다	I can make a snowman in winter. 나는 겨울에 눈사람을 만들 수 있어.

B Read, write, and say.

Read Write Say

1 see many flowers
많은 꽃을 보다

2 have a picnic
소풍을 가다

3 eat watermelon
수박을 먹다

4 swim at the beach
해변에서 수영을 하다

5 go camping
캠핑을 가다

6 see colorful leaves
알록달록한 잎들을 보다

7 enjoy winter sports
겨울 스포츠를 즐기다

8 make a snowman
눈사람을 만들다

Learn More

spring 봄	**summer** 여름	**fall** 가을	**winter** 겨울
season 계절	**vacation** 방학	**beautiful** 아름다운	**ice fishing** 얼음낚시

UNIT 6

Where Is the Bakery?

A Listen and repeat. 71 72

go straight 곧장 가다	Go straight. 곧장 가세요.
turn left 왼쪽으로 돌다	Turn left at the bookstore. 서점에서 왼쪽으로 도세요.
turn right 오른쪽으로 돌다	Turn right at the museum. 박물관에서 오른쪽으로 도세요.
on your left 당신의 왼쪽에	The park is on your left. 공원은 당신의 왼쪽에 있어요.
on your right 당신의 오른쪽에	The post office is on your right. 우체국은 당신의 오른쪽에 있어요.
one block 한 블록	Go straight one block. 한 블록 곧장 가세요.
two blocks 두 블록	Go straight two blocks and turn left. 두 블록 곧장 가서 왼쪽으로 도세요.

B Read, write, and say.

☐ Read ☐ Write ☐ Say

1 go straight
곧장 가다

2 turn left
왼쪽으로 돌다

3 turn right
오른쪽으로 돌다

4 on your left
당신의 왼쪽에

5 on your right
당신의 오른쪽에

6 one block
한 블록

7 two blocks
두 블록

Learn More

next to
~ 옆에

The toy car is next to the camera.
장난감 자동차는 카메라 옆에 있어.

between
~ 사이에

The kite is between the robot and the ball.
연은 로봇과 공 사이에 있어.

in front of
~ 앞에

The teddy bear is in front of the ball.
곰 인형은 공 앞에 있어.

behind
~ 뒤에

The robot is behind the toy car.
로봇은 장난감 자동차 뒤에 있어.

UNIT 7

Why Are You So Happy?

A Listen and repeat. 85 86

got a present 선물을 받았다	I got a present. 나는 선물을 받았어.
lost my cell phone 내 휴대 전화를 잃어버렸다	I lost my cell phone. 나는 내 휴대 전화를 잃어버렸어.
won the game 경기에서 이겼다	My team won the game. 내 팀이 경기에서 이겼어.
lost the game 경기에서 졌다	He lost the game. 그는 경기에서 졌어.
broke my glasses 내 안경을 깨뜨렸다	My cat broke my glasses. 내 고양이가 내 안경을 깨뜨렸어.
have a math test 수학 시험이 있다	We have a math test next week. 우리는 다음 주에 수학 시험이 있어.
excited 신이 난	He's excited because he got a new bike. 그는 새 자전거가 생겼기 때문에 신이 났어.
upset 화가 난	I'm upset because I broke my watch. 나는 내 시계를 망가뜨렸기 때문에 화가 났어.
worried 걱정하는	Why are they so worried? 그들은 왜 그렇게 걱정하니?

Ⓑ Read, write, and say.

☐ Read ☐ Write ☐ Say

1 got a present
선물을 받았다

2 lost my cell phone
내 휴대 전화를 잃어버렸다

3 won the game
경기에서 이겼다

4 lost the game
경기에서 졌다

5 broke my glasses
내 안경을 깨뜨렸다

6 have a math test
수학 시험이 있다

7 excited
신이 난

8 upset
화가 난

9 worried
걱정하는

Learn More

happy 행복한	I'm happy because I won the game. 나는 경기에서 이겼기 때문에 행복해.
sad 슬픈	Why are you so sad? 너는 왜 그렇게 슬퍼하니?
fixed 고쳤다	Dad fixed my drone. 아빠가 내 드론을 고치셨다.

UNIT 8

I'm Going to Go Shopping

A Listen and repeat. 99 100

go shopping 쇼핑을 하러 가다	She's going to go shopping. 그녀는 쇼핑을 하러 갈 거야.
meet my friend 내 친구를 만나다	I'm going to meet my friend. 나는 내 친구를 만날 거야.
see a musical 뮤지컬을 보다	I'm going to see a musical tomorrow. 나는 내일 뮤지컬을 볼 거야.
get a haircut 머리를 자르다	She's going to get a haircut. 그녀는 머리를 자를 거야.
visit the museum 박물관을 방문하다	I'm going to visit the museum. 나는 박물관을 방문할 거야.
practice the piano 피아노를 연습하다	Amy's going to practice the piano. 에이미는 피아노를 연습할 거야.
finish my art project 내 미술 과제를 끝내다	I'm going to finish my art project. 나는 내 미술 과제를 끝낼 거야.
plant trees 나무를 심다	He's going to plant trees this weekend. 그는 이번 주말에 나무를 심을 거야.
go to the bookstore 서점에 가다	They're going to go to the bookstore. 그들은 서점에 갈 거야.
go sledding 썰매를 타러 가다	We're going to go sledding. 우리는 썰매를 타러 갈 거야.

Ⓑ Read, write, and say.

☐ Read ☐ Write ☐ Say

1 go shopping
쇼핑을 하러 가다

2 meet my friend
내 친구를 만나다

3 see a musical
뮤지컬을 보다

4 get a haircut
머리를 자르다

5 visit the museum
박물관을 방문하다

6 practice the piano
피아노를 연습하다

7 finish my art project
내 미술 과제를 끝내다

8 plant trees
나무를 심다

9 go to the bookstore
서점에 가다

10 go sledding
썰매를 타러 가다

Learn More

tomorrow 내일	this afternoon 오늘 오후에	this evening 오늘 저녁에
at night 밤에	this weekend 이번 주말에	next weekend 다음 주말에
after school 방과 후에	map 지도	wonderful 멋진, 훌륭한

5B

Workbook

UNIT 1
Do You Want to Feed the Rabbits?

Words

Ⓐ Look and write the letter.

ⓐ see pandas ⓑ ride a horse ⓒ jump rope
ⓓ go on a trip ⓔ stay home ⓕ feed the sheep

1 

2 

3 

4 

5 

6 

Ⓑ Look, circle, and write.

1 

Do you want to ______________________?
(take a walk / stay home)

2 

Do you want to ______________________?
(see pandas / go to the aquarium)

3 

Do you want to ______________________?
(feed the rabbits / ride a horse)

Practice

Ⓐ Look and match.

1 

2 

3 

ⓐ A: Do you want to see pandas?
B: Yes, I do.

ⓑ A: Do you want to stay home?
B: No, I don't.

ⓒ A: Do you want to go on a trip?
B: Yes, I do.

ride a horse	take a walk
feed the sheep	jump rope

Ⓑ Look, write, and circle.

1 

A: Do you want to ______________?
B: (Yes, I do. / No, I don't.)

2 

A: Do you want to ______________?
B: (Yes, I do. / No, I don't.)

3 

A: Do you want to ______________?
B: (Yes, I do. / No, I don't.)

4 

A: Do you want to ______________?
B: (Yes, I do. / No, I don't.)

Write & Talk

Ⓐ Read and write the letter.

Tim: What do you want to do this vacation?

Ann: ______( )______ I want to go to China.

Tim: What do you want to do there?

Ann: ______( )______

Tim: Do you want to feed them?

Ann: ______( )______ It will be fun.

ⓐ I want to see pandas.
ⓑ Sure, I do.
ⓒ I want to go on a trip.

Ⓑ Look and write.

1

A: Do you ________ go to the ________?

B: Yes, I do. I want to see fish.

2

A: Do you want to ____________?

B: No, I ________. I'm scared.

3

A: ________ he want to ________ home?

B: Yes, he does.

4

A: Does she want ____________?

B: No, ____________.

Reading

Ⓐ Read and write.

go to the aquarium	to see
want to do	don't want to

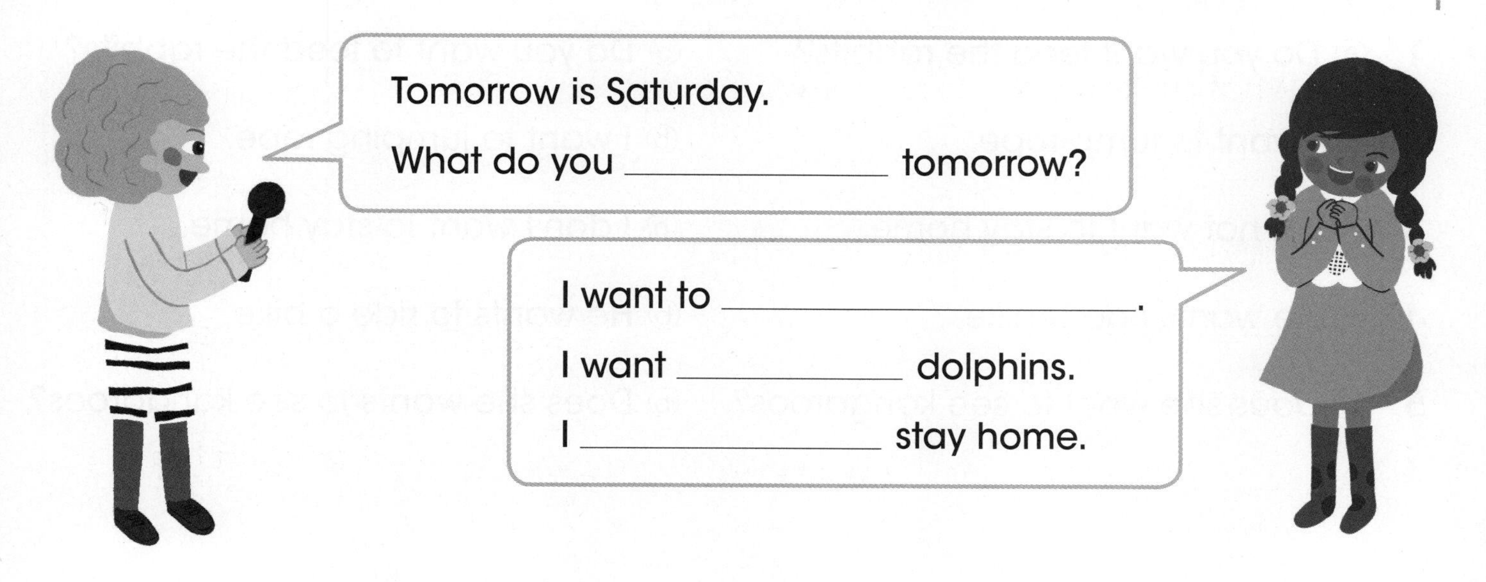

Ⓑ Read and match.

1

A: What do you want to do this summer?
B: I want to go to Australia.
I want to eat steak there.

2

A: What do you want to do this vacation?
B: I want to go to China.
I want to see pandas there.

3

A: I want to stay home.
B: What do you want to do at home?
A: I want to sleep.

ⓐ 

ⓑ 

ⓒ 

Ⓐ Choose the correct one.

1 ⓐ Do you want feed the rabbits? ⓑ Do you want to feed the rabbits?

2 ⓐ I want to jump rope. ⓑ I want to jumping rope.

3 ⓐ I'm not want to stay home. ⓑ I don't want to stay home.

4 ⓐ He wants ride a bike. ⓑ He wants to ride a bike.

5 ⓐ Does she want to see kangaroos? ⓑ Does she wants to see kangaroos?

Ⓑ Change and rewrite.

1

I **want go** to the aquarium.

⋯› ______________________________

2

Do you **want feed** the sheep?

⋯› ______________________________

3

Jane **want to** take a walk.

⋯› ______________________________

4

Does she **wants to** go on a trip?

⋯› ______________________________

Ⓐ Make the sentence.

1 ______________________________

(a horse / you / do / want / to ride / ?) 너는 말을 타고 싶니?

2 ______________________________

(he / pandas / to see / want / does / ?) 그는 판다들을 보고 싶어 하니?

3 ______________________________

(do / want / to do / what / you / there / ?) 너는 거기에서 무엇을 하고 싶니?

4 ______________________________

(I / to go on / a trip / want / .) 나는 여행을 가고 싶어.

5 ______________________________

(fish / to see / I / want / .) 나는 물고기들을 보고 싶어.

6 ______________________________

(he / to ride / wants / a bike / .) 그는 자전거를 타고 싶어 해.

7 ______________________________

(to stay / I / home / don't / want / .) 나는 집에 머물고 싶지 않아.

UNIT 2

It Has a Pink Heart

Words

A Look and check.

1

☐ yellow stars
☐ a long tail

2

☐ black stripes
☐ a small basket

3

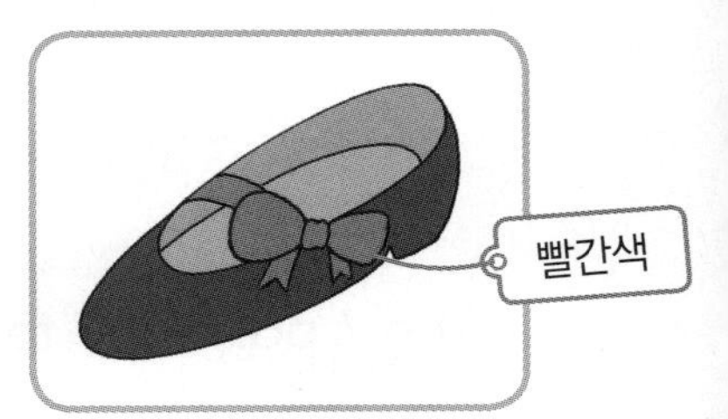

☐ two wings
☐ a red ribbon

4

☐ black stripes
☐ a big pocket

5

☐ a red ribbon
☐ two wings

6

☐ a small basket
☐ a long tail

B Look, circle, and write.

1

It has ____________________.
(a big star / a small basket)

2

It has ____________________.
(a red ribbon / a short tail)

3

It has ____________________.
(blue stripes / yellow stars)

Practice

Ⓐ Look and write.

yellow stars	two wings
black stripes	a big pocket

1

A: I can't find my sweater.

B: What does it look like?

A: It has ________________.

2

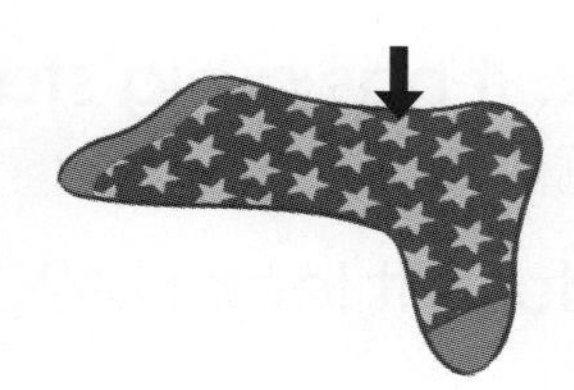

A: I can't find my sock.

B: What does it look like?

A: It has ________________.

3

A: I can't find my bag.

B: What does it look like?

A: It has ________________.

4

A: I can't find my cap.

B: What does it look like?

A: It has ________________.

Ⓑ Read and write the letter.

ⓐ

ⓑ

ⓒ

ⓓ

1

A: What does it look like?

B: It has yellow hearts. ☐

2

A: What does it look like?

B: It has red stripes. ☐

3

A: What does it look like?

B: It has a big basket. ☐

4

A: What does it look like?

B: It has a pink ribbon. ☐

Write & Talk

Ⓐ Number in the order.

☐ It's pink. It has a big star.

☐ What does it look like?

☐ I bought a new backpack.

☐ Oh, my backpack has stars, too.
I like stars.

Ⓑ Look and write.

yellow	red	cup	white stars
a pink heart	umbrella	yellow stripes	

1

A: I bought a new ________.

B: What does it look like?

A: It's blue. It has ______________.

2

A: I bought a new jacket.

B: What does it look like?

A: It's ________. It has ______________.

3

A: I bought a new ________.

B: What does it look like?

A: It's ________. It has ______________.

Reading

Ⓐ Read and write.

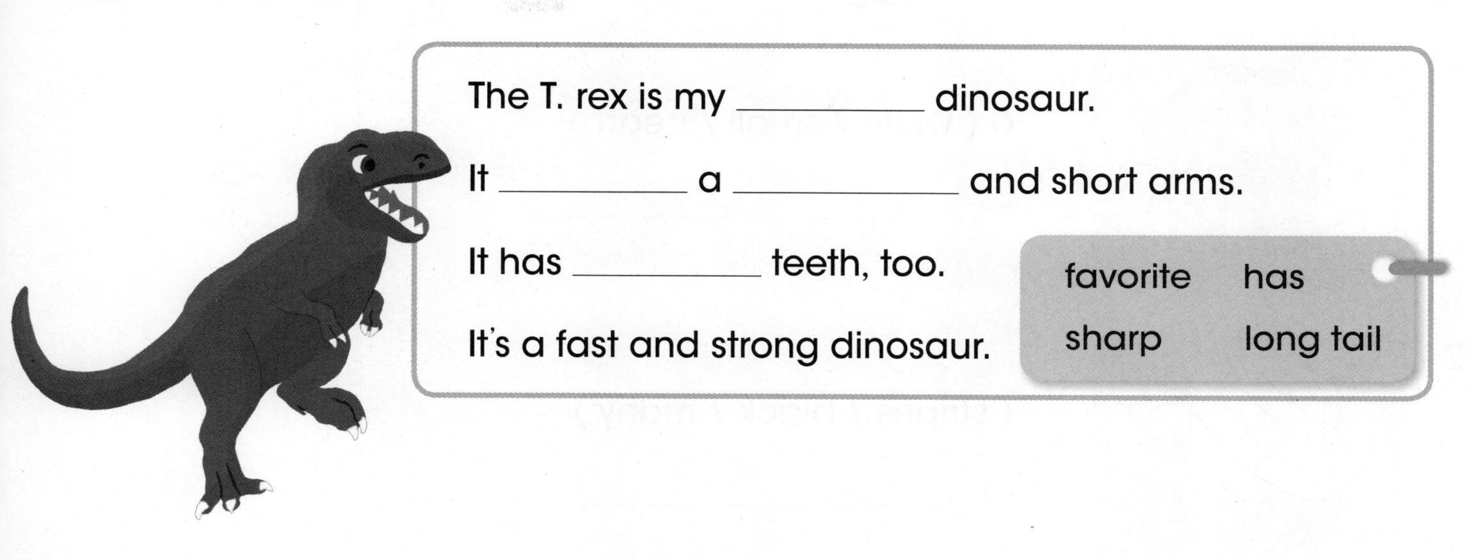

The T. rex is my ________ dinosaur.

It ________ a ________ and short arms.

It has ________ teeth, too.

It's a fast and strong dinosaur.

favorite	has
sharp	long tail

Ⓑ Look and choose.

1

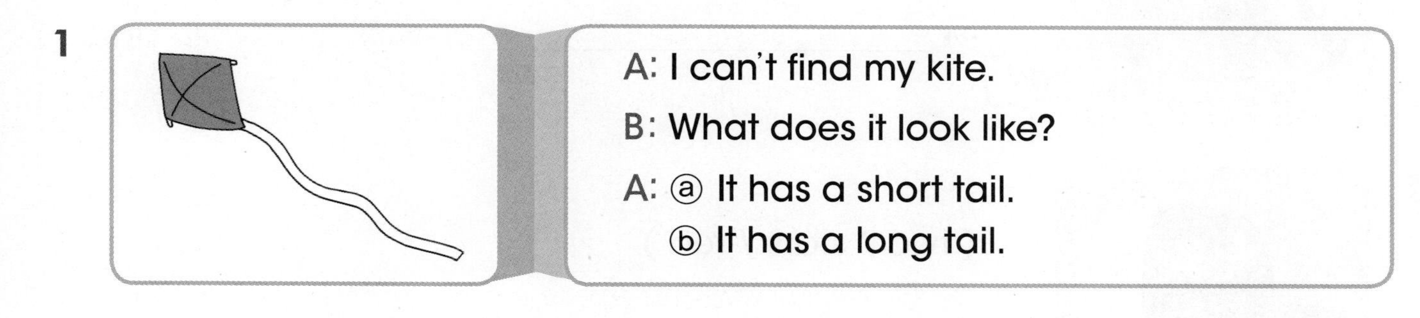

A: I can't find my kite.

B: What does it look like?

A: ⓐ It has a short tail.

ⓑ It has a long tail.

2

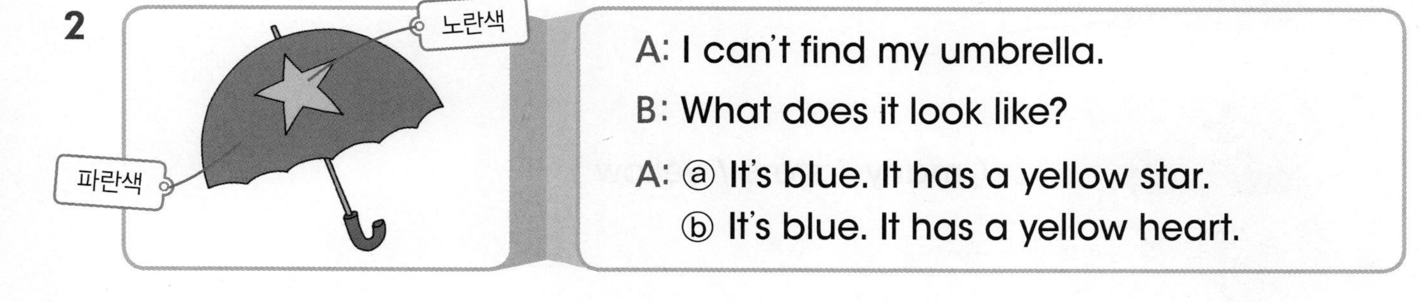

A: I can't find my umbrella.

B: What does it look like?

A: ⓐ It's blue. It has a yellow star.

ⓑ It's blue. It has a yellow heart.

3

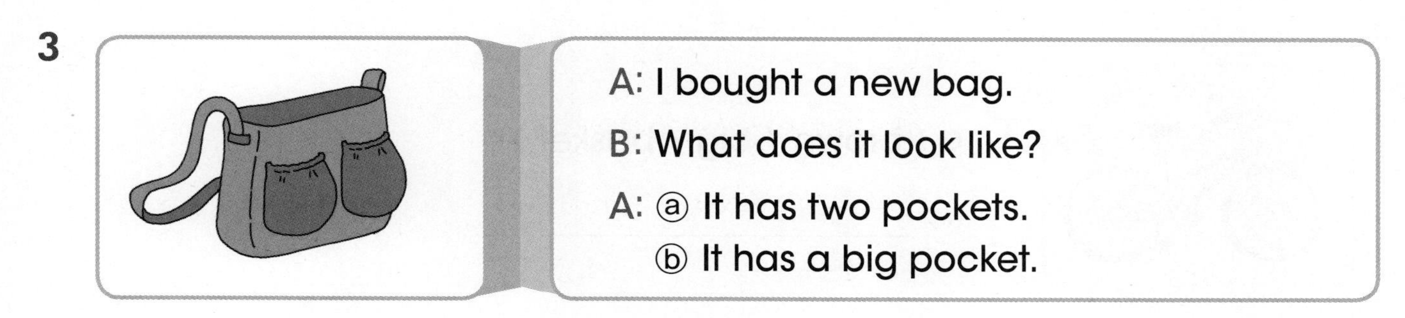

A: I bought a new bag.

B: What does it look like?

A: ⓐ It has two pockets.

ⓑ It has a big pocket.

Build Up

Ⓐ Unscramble and write.

1 흰색

a (white / small / heart)

···› ______________________

2 검은색

(stripes / black / many)

···› ______________________

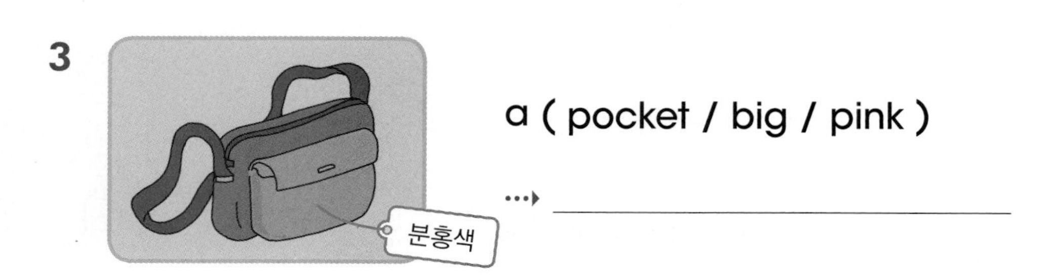

3 a (pocket / big / pink)

···› ______________________

4 (two / stars / red)

···› ______________________

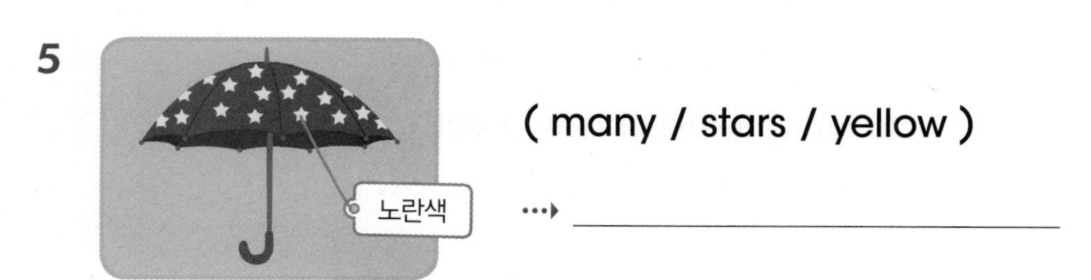

5 (many / stars / yellow)

···› ______________________

6 a (brown / big / basket)

···› ______________________

Ⓐ Make the sentence.

1 ________________________________

(lost / I / umbrella / my / .) 나는 내 우산을 잃어버렸어.

2 ________________________________

(does / it / what / like / look / ?) 그것은 어떻게 생겼니?

3 ________________________________

(pink / a / heart / it / has / .) 그것은 분홍색 하트 모양이 있어.

4 ________________________________

(red / has / a / it / ribbon / .) 그것은 빨간색 리본이 있어.

5 ________________________________

(has / backpack / too / stars / my / , / .) 내 책가방에도 별 모양들이 있어.

6 ________________________________

(stripes / it / yellow / has / two / .) 그것은 두 개의 노란색 줄무늬가 있어.

7 ________________________________

(a long tail / it / has / and / short arms / .) 그것은 긴 꼬리와 짧은 팔들을 가지고 있어.

UNIT 3

I Had a Pajama Party

Words

Ⓐ Look and write the letter.

ⓐ joined a ski camp ⓑ watched a baseball game ⓒ went fishing
ⓓ had a barbecue party ⓔ went to a concert ⓕ read a comic book

1  ☐

2  ☐

3  ☐

4  ☐

5  ☐

6 

☐

Ⓑ Look and check.

1 

I went to a concert.

It was ☐ boring.
☐ exciting.

2 

I went fishing.

It was ☐ fun.
☐ boring.

3 

I read a comic book.

It was ☐ boring.
☐ fun.

Practice

(A) Write and circle.

went to a concert	had a barbecue party
joined a ski camp	

1

I ______________________.

It was (great / boring).

2

I ______________________.

It was (fun / boring).

3

I ______________________.

It was (boring / fun).

(B) Look and choose.

1

I went fishing.

ⓐ It was fun.
ⓑ It was boring.

2

I watched a baseball game.

ⓐ It was boring.
ⓑ It was exciting.

3

ⓐ I had a barbecue party.
ⓑ I went to a concert.

It was great.

4

ⓐ I had a pajama party.
ⓑ I joined a ski camp.

It was fun.

Write & Talk

Ⓐ Read and write the letter.

Bob: What ____( )____ you do last weekend?

Tina: I ____( )____ the science museum.

Bob: What did you do there?

Tina: I ____( )____.

Bob: How was the movie?

Tina: It was ____( )____.

ⓐ went to
ⓑ did
ⓒ exciting
ⓓ saw a 4D science movie

Ⓑ Read and write T or F.

1

A: I read a comic book yesterday.

B: How was it?

A: It was boring. ☐

2

A: I joined a ski camp.

B: How was the camp?

A: It was great. ☐

3

A: What did you do last weekend?

B: I went to a concert.

A: How was it?

B: It was exciting. ☐

Reading

A Read and write.

watched a basketball game	swam
exciting	went camping	fun time

1

I ________________ with my family last weekend.

We ____________ at the lake together.

We made a campfire at night.

It was great.

2

I ________________________________ with my friends.

The game was very ____________.

Our team won the game.

We had a ____________.

B Read and match.

1

A: I watched a baseball game on Sunday.

B: How was it?

A: It was exciting.

ⓐ 

2

A: I read a comic book yesterday.

B: How was it?

A: It was boring.

ⓑ 

3

A: What did you do last weekend?

B: I went fishing.

A: How was it? B: It was fun.

ⓒ 

Build Up

A Read and circle.

1 How (was / were) the movie?

2 It (was / were) boring.

3 How (was / were) the apples?

4 They (was / were) great.

5 The soccer game (was / were) exciting.

B Complete the dialog.

1

A: How was the soccer game?

B: __________ __________ fun.

2

A: How __________ the ski camp?

B: It was exciting.

3

A: __________ __________ the fries?

B: They were salty.

4

A: I went fishing yesterday.

B: How was it?

A: __________ __________ boring.

Ⓐ Make the sentence.

1 ______________________________

(last weekend / did / you / what / do / ?) 너는 지난 주말에 무엇을 했니?

2 ______________________________

(had / we / fun time / a / .) 우리는 재미있는 시간을 보냈어.

3 ______________________________

(I / a / comic book / read / .) 나는 만화책을 읽었어.

4 ______________________________

(I / last weekend / went camping / with my family / .)
나는 지난 주말에 나의 가족들과 함께 캠핑을 갔어.

5 ______________________________

(watched / a baseball game / I / last Saturday / .)
나는 지난주 토요일에 야구 경기를 보았어.

6 ______________________________

(boring / was / it / .) 그것은 지루했어.

7 ______________________________

(the game / exciting / was / very / .) 그 경기는 매우 흥미진진했어.

UNIT 4

I Have a Stomachache

Words

A Look and check.

1

☐ cold
☐ headache

2

☐ headache
☐ toothache

3

☐ cold
☐ stomachache

4

☐ fever
☐ runny nose

5

☐ toothache
☐ stomachache

6

☐ runny nose
☐ fever

B Look and write.

some warm water	see a doctor
some medicine	some rest

1

Get ______________________.

2

Go and ______________________.

3

Take ______________________.

4

Drink ______________________.

Practice

A Look, circle, and write.

1

I have a ____________.

(toothache / cold)

2

I have a ____________.

(headache / runny rose)

3

I have a ____________.

(stomachache / fever)

B Look, write, and check.

fever runny nose toothache

1

A: I have a ____________.

B: ☐ Go and see a dentist.

☐ Take some medicine.

2

A: I have a ____________.

B: ☐ Get some rest.

☐ Drink some warm water.

3

A: I have a ____________.

B: ☐ Go and see a dentist.

☐ Get some rest.

Write & Talk

Ⓐ Read and choose.

1 A: What's wrong?
B: I have a cold.
A: Take some medicine.

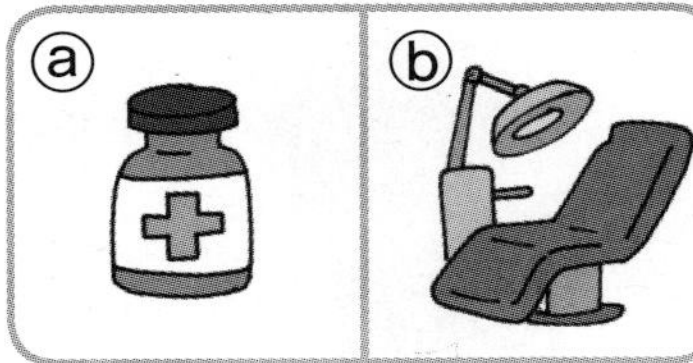

---

2 A: What's wrong?
B: I have a stomachache.
A: Drink some warm water.

---

3 A: What's wrong?
B: I have a fever.
A: Get some rest.

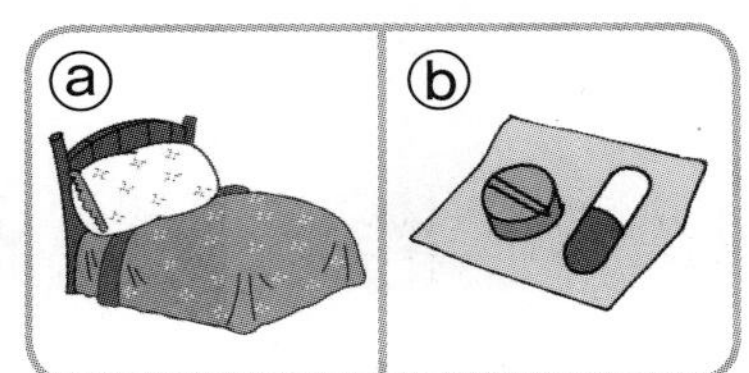

Ⓑ Look, write, and match.

①

②

③

1 I have a ____________. •

2 I have a ____________. •

3 I have a ____________. •

ⓐ • Drink some warm water.

ⓑ • Go and see a dentist.

ⓒ • Take some medicine.

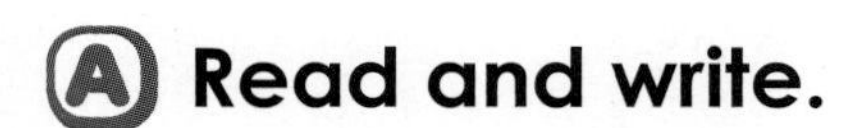

Ⓐ Read and write.

medicine　have　get some rest
runny nose　some warm water

Hello, I'm Elsa.

I'm twelve years old.

I ________ a fever.

I have a ____________, too.

Do I have a cold?

Yes, Elsa. You have a cold.

Take some __________ and

________________.

Drink ________________, too.

Don't go outside today.

Ⓑ Look, circle, and write.

1

A: What's wrong?

B: I have a (toothache / headache).

A: ______________________

2

A: What's wrong?

B: I have a (runny nose / stomachache).

A: ______________________

3

A: What's wrong?

B: I have a (cold / fever).

A: ______________________

Take some medicine.　Drink some warm water.　Go and see a doctor.

Build Up

Ⓐ Read and circle.

1 You (look / have) happy.

2 I (look / have) a toothache.

3 Tommy (looks / has) a fever.

4 The cookie (looks / has) delicious.

5 The book (looks / has) very old.

Ⓑ Look and complete.

have	has	look	looks

1

I __________ a stomachache.

2

He __________ angry.
His brother broke his robot.

3

He __________ sick. He __________ a runny nose.

4

A: She __________ sick. What's wrong?
B: She __________ a headache.

5

A: You __________ tired.
B: I __________ a lot of homework today.

Ⓐ Make the sentence.

1 ______________________________

(a stomachache / I / have / .) 나는 배가 아파.

2 ______________________________

(I / a fever / have / too / , / .) 나는 열도 있어.

3 ______________________________

(has / a runny nose / she / .) 그녀는 콧물이 나.

4 ______________________________

(drink / warm water / some / .) 따뜻한 물을 마셔라.

5 ______________________________

(and / see / go / a dentist / .) 치과에 가라.

6 ______________________________

(this medicine / take / go to bed / early / and / .)
이 약을 먹고 일찍 잠자리에 들어라.

7 ______________________________

(don't / outside / today / go / .) 오늘은 밖에 나가지 마라.

UNIT 5

What Season Do You Like?

Words

Ⓐ Look and write the letter.

ⓐ see many flowers	ⓑ have a picnic	ⓒ eat watermelon
ⓓ go camping	ⓔ see colorful leaves	ⓕ make a snowman

1 

2 

3 

4 

5 

6 

Ⓑ Look and check.

1 

☐ have a picnic
☐ eat watermelon

2 

☐ see many flowers
☐ swim at the beach

3 

☐ enjoy winter sports
☐ make a snowman

4 

☐ see colorful leaves
☐ go camping

Practice

Ⓐ Look and write.

have a picnic	see colorful leaves
make a snowman	

1 

I like fall because I can ______________________.

2 

I like spring because I can ______________________.

3 

I like winter because I can ______________________.

Ⓑ Look and write T or F.

1 

A: What season do you like?

B: I like spring because I can see many flowers. ☐

2 

A: What season do you like?

B: I like summer because I can eat watermelon. ☐

3 

A: What season do you like?

B: I like fall because I can go camping. ☐

Write & Talk

Ⓐ Look and check.

1

A: What season do you like?

B: I like winter ☐ because I can enjoy winter sports.
☐ because I can make a snowman.

2

A: What season do you like?

B: I like fall ☐ because I can go camping.
☐ because I can see colorful leaves.

3

A: What season do you like?

B: I like spring ☐ because I can eat watermelon.
☐ because I can have a picnic.

Ⓑ Look and write.

1

I like fall because I can ______________.

2

I like summer __________ I can ______________.

3

I like spring because I can __________ many __________.

Reading

Ⓐ Read and write the letter.

ⓐ to go swimming　ⓑ summer　ⓒ cold and snowy
ⓓ enjoy winter sports　ⓔ swim at the beach

It's August. It's ( ) now.
It's hot and sunny today.
I like summer because I can ( ).
I like ( ).

It's winter here. It's ( ) today.
I like winter because I can ( ).
I like skiing and ice fishing.

Ⓑ Look, circle, and write.

1

A: What season do you like?
B: I like spring because I can ________.
(see many flowers / eat watermelon)

2

A: What season do you like?
B: I like spring because I can ________.
(swim at the beach / have a picnic)

3

A: What season do you like?
B: I like fall because I can ________.
(see colorful leaves / go camping)

Ⓐ Connect and write.

I like summer. / I can go swimming.

···› I like summer because I can go swimming.

1

We like Harry. / He's funny.

···› ____________________

2

I don't like summer. / It's too hot.

···› ____________________

3

I like spring. / I can have a picnic.

···› ____________________

4

He doesn't like the book. / It's boring.

···› ____________________

5

She likes basketball. / She can jump high.

···› ____________________

Ⓐ Make the sentence.

1 ______________________________

(season / like / do / you / what / ?) 너는 무슨 계절을 좋아하니?

2 ______________________________

(because / I like / summer / in summer / my birthday / is / .)
나는 내 생일이 여름에 있기 때문에 여름을 좋아해.

3 ______________________________

(fall / I like / I can / because / go camping / .)
나는 캠핑을 갈 수 있기 때문에 가을을 좋아해.

4 ______________________________

(I like / because / winter sports / I can / winter / enjoy / .)
나는 겨울 스포츠를 즐길 수 있기 때문에 겨울을 좋아해.

5 ______________________________

(summer / I don't like / too hot / it's / because / .)
나는 너무 덥기 때문에 여름을 좋아하지 않아.

6 ______________________________

(fall / favorite / my / season is / .) 내가 가장 좋아하는 계절은 가을이야.

7 ______________________________

(have / we / too / winter vacation / , / .) 겨울 방학도 있어.

UNIT 6

Where Is the Bakery?

Words

A Look and match.

1

2

3

ⓐ go straight

ⓑ turn right

ⓒ turn left

B Look, circle, and write.

1
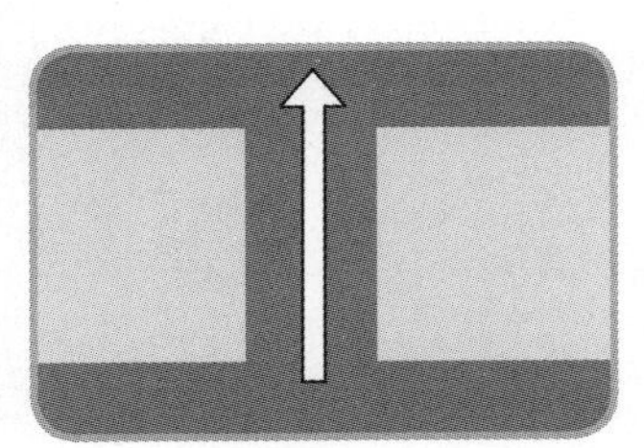

__________ one block.
(Go straight / Turn left)

2
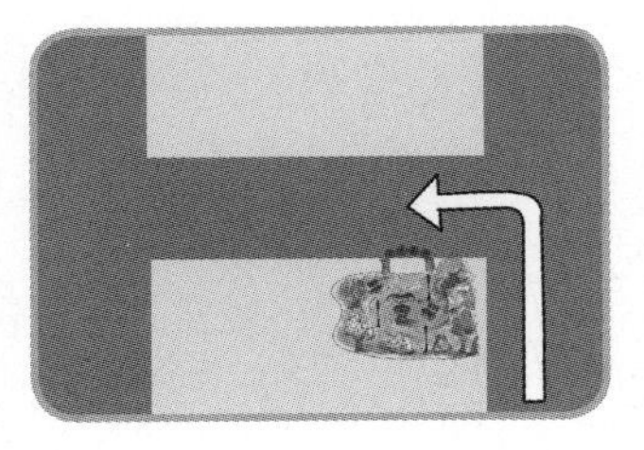

__________ at the park.
(Turn left / Turn right)

3
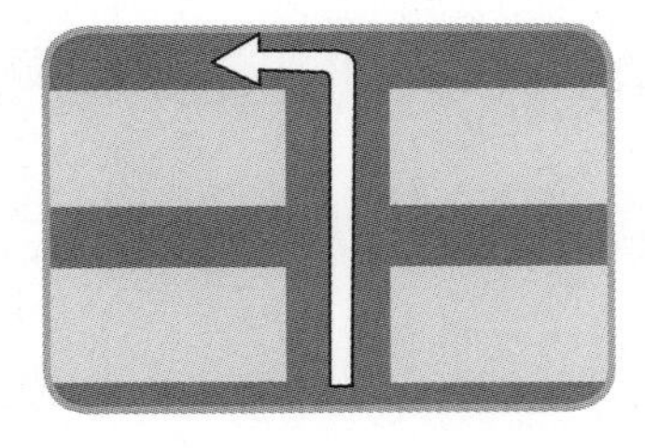

Go straight __________ and turn left.
(one block / two blocks)

Practice

Ⓐ Look and choose.

1

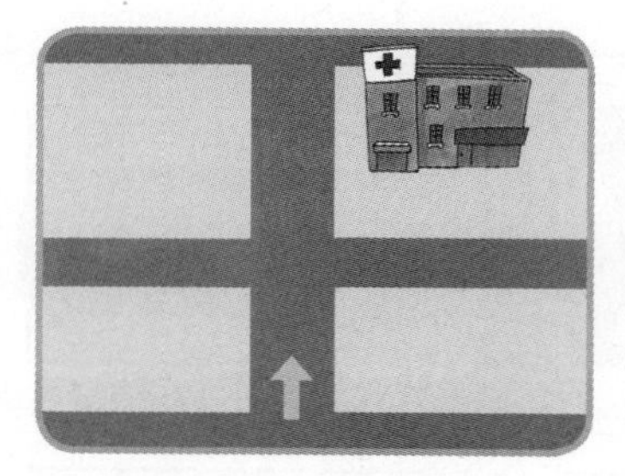

A: Where is the hospital?

B: ⓐ Go straight one block and turn right.

ⓑ Go straight two blocks and turn right.

2

A: Where is the library?

B: Go straight one block and turn right.

ⓐ It's on your left.

ⓑ It's on your right.

Ⓑ Look and write.

1

A: Where is the bakery?

B: Go straight ____________ and turn left. It's on your left.

2

A: Where is the library?

B: Go straight two blocks and ____________. It's on your left.

3

A: Where is the fire station?

B: Go straight ____________ and turn left. It's on your ________.

4

A: Where is the park?

B: Go straight two blocks and ____________. It's on your right.

Write & Talk

Ⓐ Read and write the letter.

ⓐ Go straight one block and turn left.
It's on your right.

ⓑ Go straight two blocks and turn right.
It's on your right.

ⓒ Go straight one block and turn right.
It's on your left.

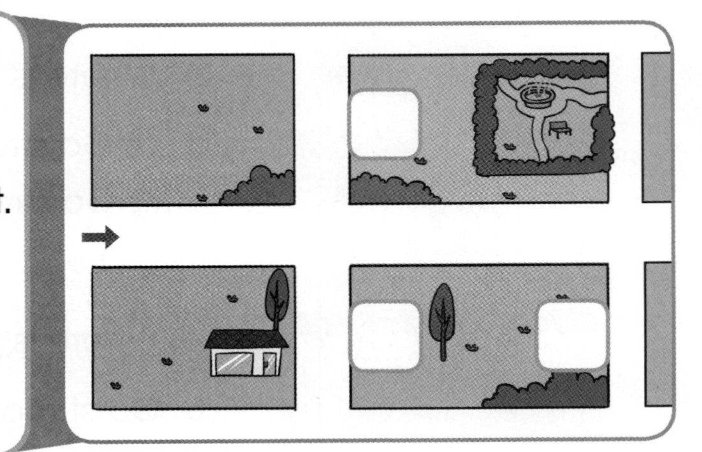

Ⓑ Read and write T or F.

1

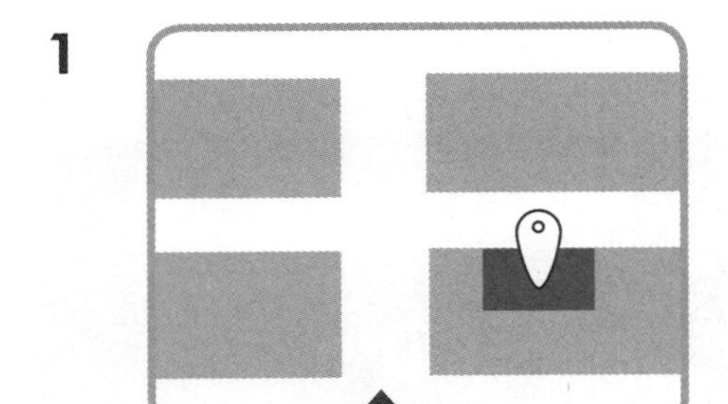

A: Where is the flower shop?
B: Go straight one block and turn right. ☐

2

A: Where is the school?
B: Go straight one block and turn left.
It's on your left. ☐

3

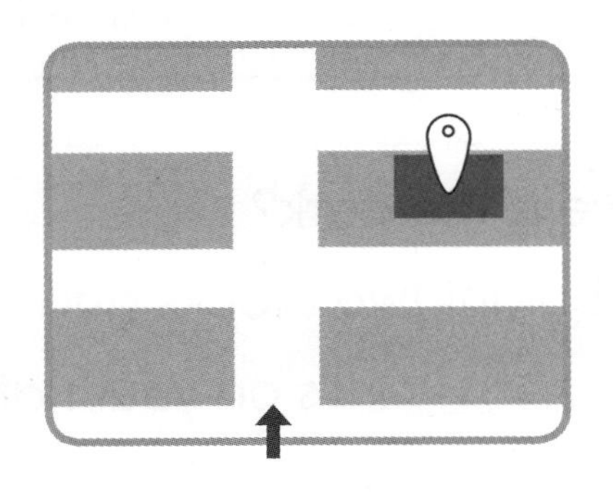

A: Where is the museum?
B: Go straight two blocks and turn left.
It's on your left. ☐

Reading

A Read and write.

How can I ____________?

Let's see. Oh, it's here.

Go straight ____________ and ____________ at the bank.

The ice cream shop is ____________ the supermarket.

I can __________ there.

I'll go with my sister. She loves ice cream, too.

walk
turn right
four blocks
get there
next to

B Look and write.

left next to right straight between

1

A: Where is the hospital?

B: Go __________ one block and turn right.

It's on your __________.

2

A: Where is the flower shop?

B: Go straight. It's __________ the post office and the park.

3

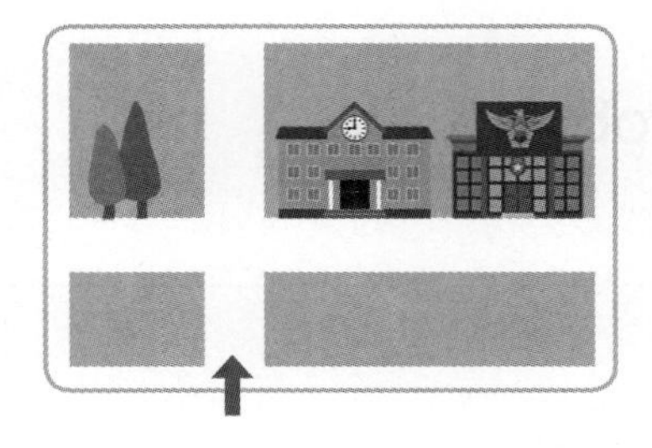

A: Where is the police station?

B: Go straight and turn __________.

It's __________ the school.

Ⓐ Change and rewrite.

1

The ball is in front of the toy car.

⋯→ The ball is ______________________.

2

The robot is behind the ball.

⋯→ The robot is ______________________.

3

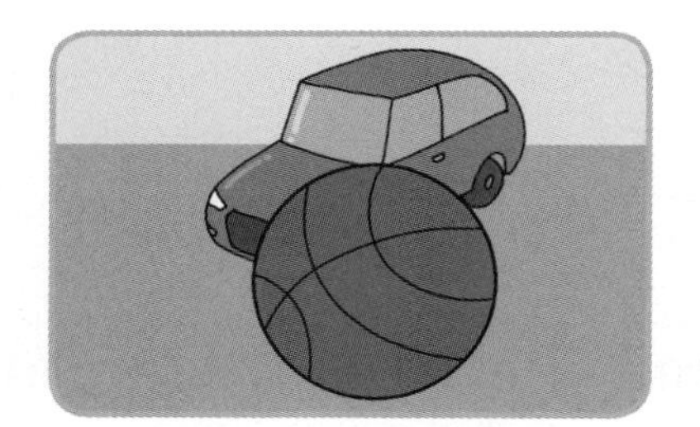

The toy car is between the robot and the ball.

⋯→ The toy car is ______________________.

4

The robot is in front of the toy car.

⋯→ The robot is ______________________.

5

The ball is next to the robot.

⋯→ The ball is ______________________.

6

The toy car is behind the robot.

⋯→ The toy car is ______________________.

Ⓐ Make the sentence.

1 ______________________________

(is / the bakery / where / ?) 빵집이 어디에 있나요?

2 ______________________________

(get to / I / can / the post office / how / ?) 우체국에 어떻게 갈 수 있나요?

3 ______________________________

(and / go / turn / straight / right / .) 곧장 가서 오른쪽으로 도세요.

4 ______________________________

(go / two blocks / straight / and / left / turn / .) 두 블록 곧장 가서 왼쪽으로 도세요.

5 ______________________________.

(and / straight / turn / right / go / at the park / .) 곧장 가서 공원에서 오른쪽으로 도세요.

6 ______________________________.

(left / it's / your / on / .) 그것은 당신의 왼쪽에 있어요.

7 ______________________________.

(between / it's / the bank / the hospital / and / .) 그것은 은행과 병원 사이에 있어요.

UNIT 7

Why Are You So Happy?

Words

A Look and check.

1

- [ ] lost the game
- [ ] broke my glasses

2

- [ ] have a math test
- [ ] got a present

3

- [ ] lost my cell phone
- [ ] broke my glasses

4

- [ ] have a math test
- [ ] won the game

5

- [ ] lost my cell phone
- [ ] won the game

6

- [ ] lost the game
- [ ] got a present

B Look and match.

1

2

3

ⓐ I got a new cell phone.

ⓑ My cat broke my watch.

ⓒ I lost my bag.

Practice

lost my cell phone　got a present
broke my glasses

Ⓐ Look, circle, and write.

1

A: Why are you so (happy / sad)?

B: I ________________.

2

A: Why are you so (sad / excited)?

B: I ________________.

3

A: Why are you so (happy / upset)?

B: I ________________.

Ⓑ Read and write the letter.

ⓐ 

ⓑ 

ⓒ 

ⓓ 

1
A: Why are you so upset?
B: I broke my glasses. ☐

2
A: Why are you so happy?
B: I got a present. ☐

3
A: Why are you so excited?
B: My team won the soccer game. ☐

4
A: Why are you so worried?
B: I have a math test tomorrow. ☐

Write & Talk

Ⓐ Number in the order.

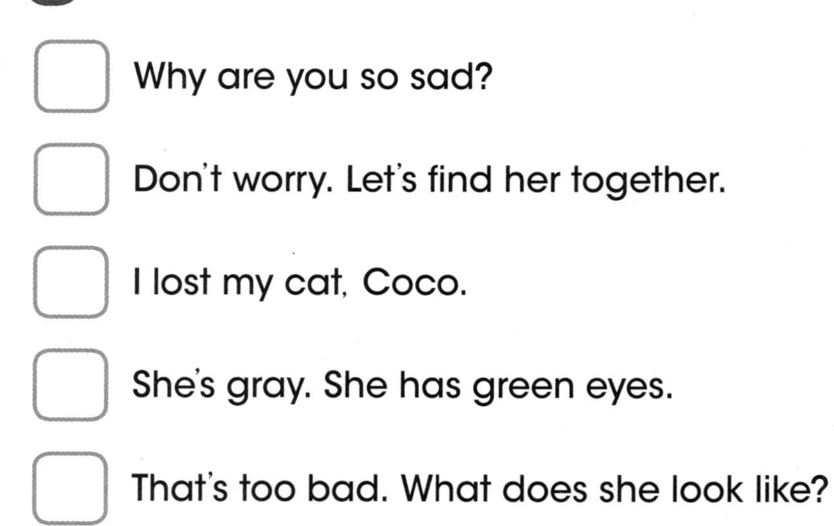

☐ Why are you so sad?

☐ Don't worry. Let's find her together.

☐ I lost my cat, Coco.

☐ She's gray. She has green eyes.

☐ That's too bad. What does she look like?

Ⓑ Look, match, and write.

broke my cup	excited	got a present

1 

ⓐ A: Why are you so happy?
B: I ______________.

2 

ⓑ A: Why are you so upset?
B: My cat ______________.

3 

ⓒ A: Why are you so __________?
B: My team won the game.

Reading

Ⓐ Read and write.

broke   excited   why   upset   got a new drone

I'm so __________ today.

__________ am I so excited?

I ____________________.

It's red and black. I want to fly it.

I went to the park with Ted.

He flew my drone and __________ it.

I was __________.

Ⓑ Look and choose.

1

A: ⓐ Why are you so worried?
ⓑ Why are you so happy?

B: I have a math test tomorrow.

A: Don't worry. I can help you.

2

A: ⓐ Why are you so excited?
ⓑ Why are you so upset?

B: I got a new bike.

A: That's great.

3

A: Why are you so upset?

B: ⓐ I lost the game.
ⓑ I won the game.

A: That's too bad.

Ⓐ Complete the sentence.

lost	made	broke
watch	math test	

1

(happy)

I'm happy ________ I got a present.

2

(upset)

I'm ________ ________ I ________ my robot.

3

(sad)

She's ________ ________ she ________ her dog.

4

(excited)

He's ________ ________ he got a new ________.

5

(worried)

They're ________ ________ they have a ________.

6

(happy)

I'm ________ ________ I ________ some new friends.

Ⓐ Make the sentence.

1 ______________________________

(are / why / happy / you / so / ?) 너는 왜 그렇게 행복해 하니?

2 ______________________________

(won / my team / yesterday / the baseball game / .)
내 팀이 어제 야구 경기에서 이겼어.

3 ______________________________

(have / I / a / tomorrow / math test / .) 나는 내일 수학 시험이 있어.

4 ______________________________

(why / so / you / are / upset / ?) 너는 왜 그렇게 화가 났니?

5 ______________________________

(drone / I / a / got / new / .) 나는 새 드론이 생겼어.

6 ______________________________

(my / broke / cat / watch / my / .) 내 고양이가 내 시계를 망가뜨렸어.

7 ______________________________

(because / happy / I'm / got / I / a present / .) 나는 선물을 받았기 때문에 행복해.

UNIT 8

I'm Going to Go Shopping

Words

Ⓐ Read and write the letter.

ⓐ 

ⓑ 

ⓒ 

ⓓ 

ⓔ 

ⓕ 

1 plant trees ☐

2 go sledding ☐

3 practice the piano ☐

4 visit the museum ☐

5 go to the bookstore ☐

6 finish my art project ☐

Ⓑ Look and write.

get a haircut	see a musical
visit the museum	

1 

I'm going to ________________.

2 

I'm going to ________________.

3 

I'm going to ________________.

Practice

Ⓐ Look, circle, and write.

1

A: What are you going to do this afternoon?

B: I'm going to ________________.

(practice the piano / go shopping)

2

A: What are you going to do this evening?

B: I'm going to ________________.

(plant trees / see a musical)

3

A: What are you going to do after school?

B: I'm going to ________________.

(go sledding / visit the museum)

Ⓑ Look and write the letter.

ⓐ
A: What are you going to do this evening?
B: I'm going to go sledding.

ⓑ
A: What are you going to do after school?
B: I'm going to finish my art project.

ⓒ
A: What are you going to do this afternoon?
B: I'm going to see a musical.

ⓓ
A: What are you going to do this evening?
B: I'm going to go to the bookstore.

1 

2 

3 

4 

Write & Talk

Ⓐ Look and choose.

1

A: What are you going to do this evening?

B: ⓐ I'm going to visit the museum.
ⓑ I'm going to see a musical.

2

A: What are you going to do this afternoon?

B: ⓐ I'm going to plant trees.
ⓑ I'm going to go to the bookstore.

3

A: What are you going to do this weekend?

B: ⓐ I'm going to go sledding.
ⓑ I'm going to finish my art project.

4

A: What are you going to do after school?

B: ⓐ I'm going to practice the violin.
ⓑ I'm going to get a haircut.

Ⓑ Read and write.

this evening	after school	this weekend
get a haircut	practice the piano	go camping

1 A: What are you going to do after school?

B: I'm going to ____________________.

2 A: What are you ______________ do ______________?

B: I'm going to get a haircut.

3 A: What are you going to do this weekend?

B: I'm going to ____________________.

Reading

Ⓐ Read and write the letter.

What is Victor ( ) ________ this weekend?

He's going to ( ) ________.

He has a good idea.

"I'm going to ( ) ________ a star map.

I'm going to watch the stars ( ) ________."

ⓐ finish his science project

ⓑ at night

ⓒ going to do

ⓓ make

Ⓑ Look and write.

1

A: What is he going to do this weekend?

B: He's going to ________.

2

A: What is Emma going to do tomorrow?

B: ________ go sledding.

3

A: What are you ________ do after school?

B: ________ plant trees.

Ⓐ Change and rewrite.

I meet my friends. (tomorrow)

···› I am going to meet my friends tomorrow.

1 

I fly my drone. (this Saturday)

···› ______________________________

2 

I play soccer. (after school)

···› ______________________________

3 

We go camping. (tomorrow)

···› ______________________________

4 

He goes to the airport. (this evening)

···› ______________________________

5 

She meets Jake. (this afternoon)

···› ______________________________

6 

They go to the zoo. (next week)

···› ______________________________

Writing

Ⓐ Make the sentence.

1 ______________________________

(after school / what / you / are / going to / do / ?)
너는 방과 후에 무엇을 할 거니?

2 ______________________________

(going to / are / you / do / there / what / ?) 너는 거기에서 무엇을 할 거니?

3 ______________________________

(do / what / is / going to / she / this weekend / ?)
그녀는 이번 주말에 무엇을 할 거니?

4 ______________________________

(I'm / go shopping / going to / .) 나는 쇼핑하러 갈 거야.

5 ______________________________

(going to / a musical / I'm / see / .) 나는 뮤지컬을 볼 거야.

6 ______________________________

(a haircut / going to / get / he's / .) 그는 머리를 자를 거야.

7 ______________________________

(finish / he's / his science project / going to / .)
그는 그의 과학 과제를 끝낼 거야.

2nd Edition
LET'S
GO
to the English World
5B